Strategic Interve...
Teacher Activity...

RtI Response to Intervention
Tier 2 Activities
Grade 4

INCLUDES:
- Diagnostic Practice for Prerequisite Skills
- Activities for Students Needing Tier 2 Instructional Intervention
- Copying Masters

Contents

SKILLS

PROBLEM SOLVING STRATEGIES

Tier 2 and Tier 3 Intervention Resources

Using the Tier 2 and Tier 3 print and online *Go Math!* Intervention Resources help students build a solid foundation of mathematical ideas and concepts. *Go Math! Response to Intervention · Tier 2 Activities* are designed for students who need small group instruction to review prerequisite concepts and skills needed for the chapter. *Go Math! Response to Intervention · Tier 3 Activities* are targeted at students who need one-on-one instruction to build foundational skills for the chapter. By focusing on essential prerequisite skills and concepts for each chapter, the tiered intervention skills prescribe instruction to prepare students to work successfully on grade-level content. The *Go Math! Response to Intervention · Tier 2 Activities, Response to Intervention · Tier 3 Activities*, and *Personal Math Trainer* resources help you accommodate the diverse skill levels of your students at all levels of intervention.

How do I determine if a student needs intervention?

Before beginning each chapter, have students complete the *Show What You Know* page in the *Go Math! Student Edition*. *Show What You Know* targets the prerequisite skills necessary for success in each chapter and allows you to diagnose a student's need for intervention. Alternatively, at the beginning of the school year, the Prerequisite Skills Test in the *Assessment Guide* can be used.

In what format are the intervention materials?

A. *Go Math! Response to Intervention · Tier 2 Activities* include the *Strategic Intervention Teacher Activity Guide*, which includes copying masters for skill development and skill practice and teacher support pages. The copying masters can be used by individual students or small groups. The teacher support pages provide teaching suggestions for skill development, as well as an Alternative Teaching Strategy for students who continue to have difficulty with a skill.

B. *Go Math! Response to Intervention · Tier 3 Activities* include the *Intensive Intervention Teacher Guide* and *Intensive Intervention Skill Packs* for Grades K-6. A separate *User Guide/Activity Guide* correlates *Intensive Intervention* Tier 3 skills and an Alternative Teaching Activity to each chapter of the *Go Math!* program.

C. *Personal Math Trainer* provides online skill development, and practice for all levels of intervention in an electronic format. *Personal Math Trainer* features pre-built assignments for intervention and practice. Students receive feedback on incorrect answers and learning aids help them develop clear insight into underlying concepts as they build toward an understanding of on-level skills.

Using Response to Intervention • Tier 2 Activities

What materials and resources do I need for intervention?

The teaching strategies may require the use of common classroom manipulatives or easily gathered classroom objects. Since these activities are designed only for those students who show weaknesses in their skill development, the quantity of materials will be small. For many activities, you may substitute materials, such as paper squares for tiles, coins for two-color counters, and so on.

How are the skill lessons in *Response to Intervention • Tier 2 Activities* structured?

Each skill lesson in the Teacher Activity Guide includes two student pages, a page of teacher support, and an answer key for the student pages.

The student lesson begins with *Learn the Math*—a guided page that provides a model or an explanation of the skill.

The second part of the lesson is *Do the Math*—a selection of exercises that provide practice and may be completed independently, with a partner, or with teacher direction. This page provides scaffolded exercises, which gradually remove prompts.

Students who have difficulty with the *Do the Math* exercises may benefit from the Alternative Teaching Strategy activity provided on the teacher support page of each lesson.

How can I organize my classroom and schedule time for intervention?

You may want to set up a Math Skill Center with a record folder for each student. Based on a student's performance on the *Show What You Know* page, assign prescribed skills by marking the student's record folder. The student can then work through the intervention materials, record the date of completion, and place the completed work in a folder for your review. Students might visit the Math Skill Center for a specified time during the day, two or three times a week, or during free time. You may wish to assign students a partner, assign a small group to work together, or work with individuals one-on-one.

Grade 4
Strategic Intervention: Response to Intervention • Tier 2
Chapter Correlations

Skill Number	Skill Title	*SWYK Chapter
9	Multiplication Facts	Multiply by 1-Digit Numbers; Factors, Multiples, and Patterns
10	Regroup Through Thousands	Multiply by 1-Digit Numbers
12	Multiply by 1-Digit Numbers	Multiply 2-Digit Numbers; Relative Sizes of Measurement Units
13	Subtract Through 4-Digit Numbers	Divide by 1-Digit Numbers
14	Subtract Through 4-Digit Numbers: Subtract Across Zeros	Divide by 1-Digit Numbers
15	Multiples	Divide by 1-Digit Numbers
18	Model Fractions and Mixed Numbers	Multiply Fractions by Whole Numbers
19	Fractions with Denominators of 10	Relate Fractions and Decimals
26	Add Whole Numbers	Algebra: Perimeter and Area
27	Multiply Whole Numbers	Algebra: Perimeter and Area
29	Equivalent Fractions	Relate Fractions and Decimals
30	Regroup Hundreds as Tens	Place Value, Addition, and Subtraction to One Million
31	2-Digit Addition and Subtraction	Place Value, Addition, and Subtraction to One Million
32	2-Digit by 1-Digit Multiplication	Multiply 2-Digit Numbers
33	Arrays	Factors, Multiples, and Patterns

*SWYK refers to the *Show What You Know* page at the beginning of each chapter.

Grade 4
Strategic Intervention: Response to Intervention • Tier 2
Chapter Correlations

Skill Number	Skill Title	*SWYK Chapter
34	Compare Parts of a Whole	Fraction Equivalence and Comparison
35	Name the Shaded Part	Fraction Equivalence and Comparison
36	Read and Write Fractions	Add and Subtract Fractions
37	Parts of a Whole	Add and Subtract Fractions; Angles
38	Read and Write Mixed Numbers	Multiply Fractions by Whole Numbers
39	Number of Sides	Two-Dimensional Figures
40	Geometric Patterns	Two-Dimensional Figures
41	Classify Angles	Angles

*SWYK refers to the *Show What You Know* page at the beginning of each chapter.

Place Value to Ten Thousand
Skill 1

Objective
To read and write numbers to ten thousand

Vocabulary
word form A way to write numbers using words

expanded form A way to write numbers by showing the value of each digit

standard form A way to write numbers by using the digits 0–9 with each digit having a place value

Manipulatives
base-ten blocks

COMMON ERROR

- Students may forget to write a 0 as a placeholder when there are no hundreds, tens, or ones.

- To correct this, remind students to write a zero (0) for each place-value position that does not have any hundreds, tens, or ones. Have students compare the model to the number written in standard form to check their answers.

Learn the Math page IN3 Review with students the different ways numbers can be written.

Guide students through the examples. Encourage students to use base-ten blocks to model each number. In Example 3, there are no tens blocks. Ask: **How can you show that there are no tens?** Possible answer: I can write a 0 in the tens place.

REASONING Have students use base-ten blocks to model both numbers and then write both numbers in standard form. Ask: **Are the numbers the same?** No; possible answer: 2,407 has 0 tens and 7 ones, and 2,470 has 7 tens and 0 ones.

Do the Math page IN4 Work through Exercise 1 with students. Ask: **How many blocks does Carlos have?** 1 thousand, 5 hundreds, 3 tens, and 2 ones Ask: **In what different forms can you write the number?** word form, standard form, and expanded form

Assign Exercises 2–11 and monitor students' work.

Discuss Problem 12. Ask: **How can you show that Molly has no ones blocks when you write the number?** Write a 0 in the ones place.

Students who make more than 3 errors in Exercises 1–12 may benefit from the **Alternative Teaching Strategy**.

Alternative Teaching Strategy
Manipulatives: base-ten blocks, paper bag, 0–9 digit cards (2 sets), place-value charts (see *Teacher Resources*)

Mix the digit cards and put them in a paper bag. Have students draw four cards from the bag without looking. Have them use the digits drawn to write a 4-digit number in the place-value chart. Then have students model their numbers using the base-ten blocks. Check that students model the number correctly. Then ask students to write their numbers in standard, expanded, and word forms. Discuss students' work. Have students return the cards to the bag and repeat the activity.

Learn the Math

You can write numbers in different ways. **Word form** is a way to write numbers using words. **Expanded form** is a way to write numbers by showing the value of each digit. **Standard form** is a way to write numbers by using the digits 0–9, with each digit having a place value.

Vocabulary

word form
expanded form
standard form

Write the number represented by the base-ten blocks three ways.

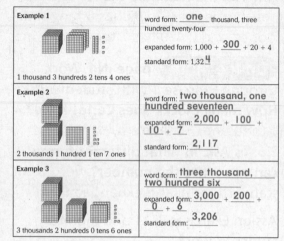

Example 1	word form: **one** thousand, three hundred twenty-four
	expanded form: 1,000 + **300** + 20 + 4
	standard form: 1,32**4**
1 thousand 3 hundreds 2 tens 4 ones	
Example 2	word form: **two thousand, one hundred seventeen**
	expanded form: **2,000** + **100** + **10** + **7**
	standard form: **2,117**
2 thousands 1 hundred 1 ten 7 ones	
Example 3	word form: **three thousand, two hundred six**
	expanded form: **3,000** + **200** + **0** + **6**
	standard form: **3,206**
3 thousands 2 hundreds 0 tens 6 ones	

REASONING Felix says that 2,000 + 400 + 70 is another way to write 2,407. What is Felix's error?

Possible answer: Felix reversed the value of the tens and ones digits. 2,407 is 2,000 + 400 + 0 + 7.

Do the Math

Skill ①

1. Carlos has the base-ten blocks shown. What are the different ways he can write the number his blocks represent?

- Write how many of each type of block Carlos has.
  1 thousand **5** hundreds **3** tens **2** ones

- Write this number in word form.
  one **thousand**, five **hundred thirty-two**

- Write this number in expanded form.
  1,000 + **500** + 30 + **2**

- Write this number in standard form. **1,532**

Remember

Use 0 as a placeholder when there are no hundreds, tens, or ones.

Complete the chart to show each number in three ways.

	Standard Form	Expanded Form	Word Form
2.	6,491	6,000 + 400 + 90 + 1	**six** thousand, **four** hundred ninety-one
3.	9,012	**9,000** + **10** + 2	nine thousand, twelve
4.	7,480	**7,000 + 400 + 80**	**seven** thousand, four hundred **eighty**
5.	4,503	4,000 + 500 + 3	four thousand, five hundred three

Find the value of the underlined digit.

6. 8,317 → **8,000**   7. 6,052 → **0**   8. 4,220 → **20**

9. 3,905 → **5**   10. 5,135 → **100**   11. 9,366 → **9,000**

12. Molly has 3 thousands blocks, 9 hundreds blocks, and 8 tens blocks. How can you write the number her blocks represent in standard form?
3,980

Name _____

Learn the Math

You can write numbers in different ways. **Word form** is a way to write numbers using words. **Expanded form** is a way to write numbers by showing the value of each digit. **Standard form** is a way to write numbers by using the digits 0–9, with each digit having a place value.

Vocabulary

word form
expanded form
standard form

Write the number represented by the base-ten blocks three ways.

Example 1 1 thousand 3 hundreds 2 tens 4 ones	word form: _____ thousand, three hundred twenty-four expanded form: 1,000 + _____ + 20 + 4 standard form: 1,32__
Example 2 2 thousands 1 hundred 1 ten 7 ones	word form: _____ _____ expanded form: _____ + _____ + _____ + ____ standard form: _____
Example 3 3 thousands 2 hundreds 0 tens 6 ones	word form: _____ _____ expanded form: _____ + _____ + _____ + ____ standard form: _____

REASONING Felix says that 2,000 + 400 + 70 is another way to write 2,407. What is Felix's error?

_____

_____

1. Carlos has the base-ten blocks shown. What are the different ways he can write the number his blocks represent?

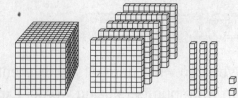

- Write how many of each type of block Carlos has.

   _____ thousand _____ hundreds _____ tens

   _____ ones

- Write this number in word form.

   one _____, five _____ _____

- Write this number in expanded form.

   1,000 + _____ + 30 + ____

- Write this number in standard form. _____

> **Remember**
> Use 0 as a placeholder when there are no hundreds, tens, or ones.

Complete the chart to show each number in three ways.

	Standard Form	Expanded Form	Word Form
2.		6,000 + 400 + 90 + 1	_____ thousand, _____ hundred ninety-one
3.		_____ + ____ + 2	nine thousand, twelve
4.	7,480		_____ thousand, four hundred _____
5.		4,000 + 500 + 3	

Find the value of the underlined digit.

6. 8,317 → _____   7. 6,052 → _____   8. 4,220 → _____

9. 3,905 → _____   10. 5,135 → _____   11. 9,366 → _____

12. Molly has 3 thousands blocks, 9 hundreds blocks, and 8 tens blocks. How can you write the number her blocks represent in standard form?

   _____

Locate Numbers
Skill 2

Objective
To locate and name points and numbers on a number line

Vocabulary
number line A line on which numbers can be located

COMMON ERROR

- Students may incorrectly count the marks on the number line.

- To correct this, have students begin at a labeled mark on the number line, draw skips, and count aloud as they move to the right.

Learn the Math page IN7 Discuss the first example with students. Ask: **What does each mark on the number line represent?** an increase of 100 **How many marks to the right of 2,500 is point X?** 2 Have students begin at 2,500 and count aloud by hundreds until they reach point X. Remind them that numbers on a number line increase as you move from left to right.

Guide students through the steps to find the numbers represented by points P and Q. Ask: **What numbers are shown on the number line?** 2,000 through 2,500 **What does each mark on the number line represent?** an increase of 10 After students locate points P and Q, ask other questions about the number line. Ask: **What number does the longer mark between 2,000 and 2,100 represent?** 2,050 **How can using the longer marks help you locate a number on the number line?**

Possible answer: I can start on one of the longer marks and count by tens as I move to the right.

REASONING Have students identify that Cedric needs to count one mark to the right of 2,300 rather than counting left.

Do the Math page IN8 Guide students through Exercise 1.

Assign Exercises 2–13 and monitor students' work. Point out that Exercises 8–13 require three steps: locate the number, draw the point, and then label the point with a letter.

Discuss Problem 14. Ask: **What is Tara's math score?** 101 **What is her reading score?** 95 **How do you find how many more points she scores in math than in reading?** Possible answer: subtract; 101 − 95 = 6 points

Students who make more than 4 errors in Exercises 1–14 may benefit from the **Alternative Teaching Strategy**.

Alternative Teaching Strategy
Materials: number lines (see *Teacher Resources*)

Have students use skip-counting patterns to locate points on a number line. Have students work in pairs. Give each pair a number line showing numbers from 1,000 to 5,000 with labels on every thousand and marks on every hundred. Discuss that each mark counts by hundreds. Have students draw skips on the number line as they count aloud from 1,000 to 5,000 by hundreds. Ask one student to draw a point on the number line and have the other student skip count to identify the number represented by the point. Have students take turns drawing the point and skip counting. Repeat the activity with other number lines.

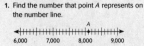

Locate Numbers
Skill ❷

Learn the Math

Omar is playing a game that uses a number line. His game piece is on the point labeled X. What number does X represent?

A number line shows numbers in order from least to greatest.

Vocabulary

number line

```
◄─┼┼┼┼┼┼┼┼┼┼┼┼┼┼┼┼┼┼┼┼─►
2,000   2,500   3,000   3,500   4,000
          X
```

This number line shows marks for numbers from 2,000 through 4,000. Each mark shown on the number line counts by hundreds. Point X is 2 marks to the right of 2,500.

So, point X represents __2,700__

Another Example

Write the number represented by each letter.

```
◄─┼┼┼┼┼┼┼┼┼┼┼┼┼┼┼┼┼┼┼┼┼┼┼─►
2,000  2,100  2,200  2,300  2,400  2,500
               P            Q
```

Point P is between ___2,100___ and ___2,200___

Each mark shown on the number line counts by tens. Point P is 6 marks to the right of 2,100.

So, point P represents __2,160__

Point Q is between ___2,300___ and ___2,400___

Point Q is __9__ marks to the right of 2,300.

So, point Q represents __2,390__

REASONING What's the error? Cedric says to locate 2,310 on the number line above, you should find 2,300 and then count left one mark. Is he correct? Explain.

No; possible answer: to locate 2,310 on the number line, Cedric should find 2,300 and then count right one mark.

Response to Intervention • Tier 2 **IN7**

Do the Math

Skill ❷

1. Find the number that point A represents on the number line.

```
            A
◄─┼┼┼┼┼┼┼┼┼┼┼┼┼┼┼┼┼┼┼┼┼─►
6,000   7,000   8,000   9,000
```

Remember
The numbers on a number line increase from left to right.

• Point A is between __8,000__ and __9,000__

• Point A is __1__ mark to the right of __8,000__

So, point A represents __8,100__

Write the number represented by each letter.

```
     A      B      C      D     E          F
◄─┼┼┼┼┼┼┼┼┼┼┼┼┼┼┼┼┼┼┼┼┼┼┼┼┼┼┼┼─►
4,500  4,600  4,700  4,800  4,900  5,000
```

2. A __4,530__   3. B __4,600__   4. C __4,680__
5. D __4,790__   6. E __4,850__   7. F __4,980__

Locate each number on the number line. Draw a point and label it with a letter.

```
  G           H      I      J   K      L
◄─┼┼┼┼┼┼┼┼┼┼┼┼┼┼┼┼┼┼┼┼┼┼┼┼┼┼─►
 800    900   1,000  1,100  1,200  1,300
```

8. G 810   9. H 950   10. I 1,040
11. J 1,120   12. K 1,170   13. L 1,260

14. Use the number line below. Point M shows Tara's math score and point R shows her reading score. How many more points does she have in math than in reading?

6 points

```
      R   M
◄─┼┼┼┼┼┼┼┼┼┼┼┼┼┼┼┼┼┼┼┼─►
 90    100   110   120
```

IN8 Response to Intervention • Tier 2

Name _____

Learn the Math

Omar is playing a game that uses a number line. His game piece is on the point labeled *X*. What number does *X* represent?

A number line shows numbers in order from least to greatest.

Vocabulary

number line

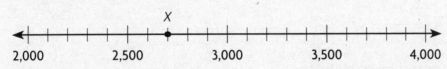

This number line shows marks for numbers from 2,000 through 4,000. Each mark shown on the number line counts by hundreds. Point *X* is 2 marks to the right of 2,500.

So, point *X* represents _____.

Another Example

Write the number represented by each letter.

Point *P* is between _____ and _____.

Each mark shown on the number line counts by tens. Point *P* is 6 marks to the right of 2,100.

So, point *P* represents _____.

Point *Q* is between _____ and _____.

Point *Q* is _____ marks to the right of 2,300.

So, point *Q* represents _____.

REASONING What's the error? Cedric says to locate 2,310 on the number line above, you should find 2,300 and then count left one mark. Is he correct? Explain.

_____

_____

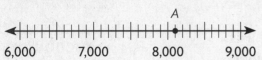

1. Find the number that point *A* represents on the number line.

• Point *A* is between _____ and _____.

• Point *A* is _____ mark to the right of _____.

So, point *A* represents _____.

Write the number represented by each letter.

2. *A* _____

3. *B* _____

4. *C* _____

5. *D* _____

6. *E* _____

7. *F* _____

Locate each number on the number line. Draw a point and label it with a letter.

8. *G* 810

9. *H* 950

10. *I* 1,040

11. *J* 1,120

12. *K* 1,170

13. *L* 1,260

14. Use the number line below. Point *M* shows Tara's math score and point *R* shows her reading score. How many more points does she have in math than in reading?

_____

Meaning of Multiplication: Equal Groups
Skill 3

Objective
To find the total number of objects using equal groups and number lines

Vocabulary
equal groups Groups that have the same number of objects

Manipulatives
counters

COMMON ERROR

- Students may try to skip count to find the total number of items in groups that are not equal.

- To correct this, model groups that are not equal using counters. Use a number line to count the number of objects in the groups. Discuss that the skips made when counting are not of equal length.

Learn the Math page IN11 Read and discuss Example 1 with students. Ask students to skip count aloud to find the total number of cookies represented by the counters.

Discuss Example 2 with students. Have them trace the skips on the number line as they make 6 jumps of 3. Ask: **On what number did you stop?** 18

REASONING Discuss the question with students. Have students model the equal groups in Example 2 with counters. Then have them arrange the counters so that they are no longer in equal groups. Ask them to count the number of counters in the groups aloud. Have students identify that they are no longer using a skip-counting pattern to count.

Do the Math page IN12 Read and discuss Exercise 1 with students. Explain that they first need to find the number of equal groups. Then they need to find how many are in each group. Guide students to skip count to find the total number of pencils that Evan has.

Assign Exercises 2–7 and monitor students' work.

Discuss Problem 8. Have students draw a number line to skip count to find the total number of marbles. Ask: **By what number should you skip count to find the total number of marbles?** 6 **How many jumps of 6 will you make?** 4 **How many marbles does Kaley have?** 24 marbles

Students who make more than 2 errors in Exercises 1–8 may benefit from the **Alternative Teaching Strategy**.

Alternative Teaching Strategy
Explain to students that they can use repeated addition to find the total number of objects in a group. Model 4 groups of 3 counters. Have students find the total number of counters in the groups using the addition sentence $3 + 3 + 3 + 3 = 12$.

Next show students a number line showing 6 jumps of 2. Ask: **What addition sentence can you write to find 6 jumps of 2?** $2 + 2 + 2 + 2 + 2 + 2 = 12$

Repeat with similar problems using both counters and number lines.

© Houghton Mifflin Harcourt Publishing Company

Name _____

Learn the Math

Leah is making cookies. She has 4 equal groups with 5 cookies in each group. How many cookies does Leah make in all?

Example 1
Use counters to model the equal groups.

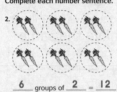

Skip count to find how many cookies Leah makes in all.

5, __10__, __15__, __20__

There are __4__ groups with __5__ cookies in each group.

So, Leah makes __20__ cookies in all.

Example 2
Use a number line to count equal groups.

Cameron has a rock collection. He puts his rocks in 6 equal groups with 3 rocks in each group. How many rocks does Cameron have in all?

Begin at 0. Draw jumps on the number line to skip count by threes.

Make __6__ jumps of __3__

```
0 1 2 3 4 5 6 7 8 9 10 11 12 13 14 15 16 17 18 19 20
```

So, Cameron has __18__ rocks in all.

REASONING If Cameron does not put his rocks in equal groups, will you be able to skip count to find how many rocks he has in all? Explain.

No; possible answer: when you skip count,
you count forward by the same number. So, the
groups need to be equal.

Response to Intervention • Tier 2 **IN11**

1. There are 4 pencils in a package. If Evan buys 3 packages of pencils, how many pencils does he have?

- How many equal groups are there? __3__
- How many are in each group? __4__
- Use counters to model 3 groups of 4.
- Skip count to find how many pencils Evan has.

  __4__, __8__, __12__

- __3__ groups of __4__ = __12__

So, Evan has __12__ pencils.

Remember
To find the total number of objects in equal groups, you can skip count by the number of objects in each group.

Complete each number sentence.

2.
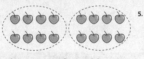

__6__ groups of __2__ = __12__

3.
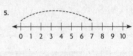

__5__ groups of __4__ = __20__

4.
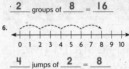

__2__ groups of __8__ = __16__

5.
```
0 1 2 3 4 5 6 7 8 9 10
```

__1__ jump of __7__ = __7__

6.
```
0 1 2 3 4 5 6 7 8 9 10
```

__4__ jumps of __2__ = __8__

7.
```
0 1 2 3 4 5 6 7 8 9 10
```

__3__ jumps of __3__ = __9__

8. Kaley has 4 bags of marbles. There are 6 marbles in each bag. How many marbles does Kaley have in all?

24 marbles

IN12 Response to Intervention • Tier 2

Name _____

Learn the Math

Leah is making cookies. She has 4 equal groups with 5 cookies in each group. How many cookies does Leah make in all?

Vocabulary

equal groups

Example 1

Use counters to model the equal groups.

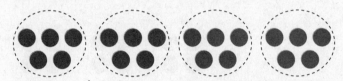

Skip count to find how many cookies Leah makes in all.

5, _____, _____, _____

There are _____ groups with _____ cookies in each group.

So, Leah makes _____ cookies in all.

Example 2

Use a number line to count equal groups.

Cameron has a rock collection. He puts his rocks in 6 equal groups with 3 rocks in each group. How many rocks does Cameron have in all?

Begin at 0. Draw jumps on the number line to skip count by threes.

Make _____ jumps of _____.

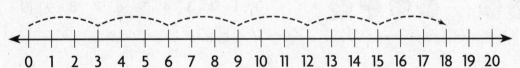

So, Cameron has _____ rocks in all.

REASONING If Cameron does not put his rocks in equal groups, will you be able to skip count to find how many rocks he has in all? Explain.

_____

_____

_____

1. There are 4 pencils in a package. If Evan buys
   3 packages of pencils, how many pencils does he have?

   • How many equal groups are there? _____

   • How many are in each group? _____

   • Use counters to model 3 groups of 4.

   • Skip count to find how many pencils Evan has.

   _____ , _____ , _____

   • _____ groups of _____ = _____

   So, Evan has _____ pencils.

> **Remember**
> To find the total number of objects in equal groups, you can skip count by the number of objects in each group.

Complete each number sentence.

2.

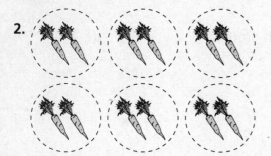

_____ groups of _____ = _____

3.

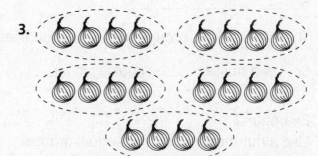

_____ groups of _____ = _____

4.

_____ groups of _____ = _____

5.

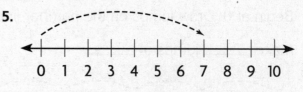

_____ jump of _____ = _____

6.

_____ jumps of _____ = _____

7.

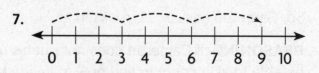

_____ jumps of _____ = _____

8. Kaley has 4 bags of marbles. There are 6 marbles in each bag.
   How many marbles does Kaley have in all?

   _____

Meaning of Multiplication: Arrays
Skill 4

Objective
To find the total number of objects in an array

Vocabulary
array A set of objects or numbers arranged in equal rows and columns

Manipulatives
square tiles, MathBoard

COMMON ERROR

- Students may reverse the rows and columns when making arrays.

- To correct this, guide students to make arrays using square tiles. Reinforce that the rows are arranged from left to right and that the columns are arranged from top to bottom.

Learn the Math page IN15 Read and discuss Example 1 with students. Ask: **How many rows are in the array?** 5 **How many tiles are in each row?** 4 Direct students to make the same array with square tiles. Ask: **How many tiles are in the array in all?** 20

Discuss Example 2 with students. Using different tiles, have students make the new array. Ask: **How many tiles are in the array in all?** 20

REASONING Discuss the question with students. Direct them to the arrays they made in Example 1 and Example 2. Have students compare the number of rows and the numbers of tiles in each row in each array. Then have them compare the total number of tiles in each array.

Do the Math page IN16 Read and discuss Exercise 1 with students. Remind them that they first need to find the number of rows. Then they need to find the number of objects in each row. Guide students to make an array to model the total number of chairs.

Assign Exercises 2–7 and monitor students' work.

Discuss Problem 8 with students. Ask: **How can you make an array to model the total number of corn plants?** Possible answer: I can make 6 rows with 9 tiles in each row. **How many tiles are in the array in all?** 54 tiles

Students who make more than 2 errors in Exercises 1–8 may benefit from the **Alternative Teaching Strategy**.

Alternative Teaching Strategy
Manipulatives: square tiles

Show students that they can skip count to find the total number of tiles in an array. Direct students to the array in Example 1. Have them skip count by the number of tiles in each row. 4, 8, 12, 16, 20 Have students skip count to find the total number of tiles in Example 2. 5, 10, 15, 20

Ask students to work in pairs. Have them use square tiles to make other arrays and skip count to find the total number of tiles in each array.

Name _____

Learn the Math

Mrs. Martin is making a poster. Her poster has 5 rows of pictures with 4 pictures in each row. How many pictures does Mrs. Martin have on her poster in all?

Example 1

Show the number of pictures using an array. An array is a set of objects or numbers arranged in equal rows and columns. Make an array with 5 rows of 4 tiles.

Count the number of tiles in the array.

__5__ rows of __4__ = __20__

So, there are __20__ pictures on Mrs. Martin's poster in all.

Example 2

If Mrs. Martin rearranges her poster to have 4 rows with 5 pictures in each row, how many pictures will she have on the poster in all? Make an array with 4 rows of 5 tiles.

__4__ rows of __5__ = __20__

So, Mrs. Martin's poster will have __20__ pictures in all.

REASONING Explain how the arrays in Example 1 and Example 2 are alike and how they are different.
Possible answer: the arrays have the same number of tiles. They are arranged differently.

Response to Intervention • Tier 2 **IN15**

Do the Math

Skill ④

1. Mr. Hall's classroom has 4 rows of chairs with 8 chairs in each row. How many chairs are there in all?
   • Use tiles to make an array.
   • How many rows of chairs are there? __4__
   • How many chairs are in each row? __8__
   • __4__ rows of __8__ = __32__
   So, Mr. Hall's classroom has __32__ chairs in all.

Complete each number sentence.

2. __1__ row of __6__ = __6__

3. __4__ rows of __9__ = __36__

4. __3__ rows of __7__ = __21__

5. __2__ rows of __4__ = __8__

6. __5__ rows of __6__ = __30__

7. __4__ rows of __8__ = __32__

8. Mrs. Rivera is growing corn in her garden. She plants 6 rows of corn plants with 9 plants in each row. How many corn plants are there in all?
   __54 corn plants__

IN16 Response to Intervention • Tier 2

Name _____

Learn the Math

Mrs. Martin is making a poster. Her poster has 5 rows of pictures with 4 pictures in each row. How many pictures does Mrs. Martin have on her poster in all?

Vocabulary

array

Example 1

Show the number of pictures using an array. An array is a set of objects or numbers arranged in equal rows and columns. Make an array with 5 rows of 4 tiles.

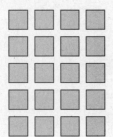

Count the number of tiles in the array.

_____ rows of _____ = _____

So, there are _____ pictures on Mrs. Martin's poster in all.

Example 2

If Mrs. Martin rearranges her poster to have 4 rows with 5 pictures in each row, how many pictures will she have on the poster in all? Make an array with 4 rows of 5 tiles.

_____ rows of _____ = _____

So, Mrs. Martin's poster will have _____ pictures in all.

REASONING Explain how the arrays in Example 1 and Example 2 are alike and how they are different.

_____

_____

IN15

1. Mr. Hall's classroom has 4 rows of chairs with 8 chairs in each row. How many chairs are there in all?

> **Remember**
> Count all the tiles in an array to find the total number of items.

- Use tiles to make an array.

- How many rows of chairs are there? _____

- How many chairs are in each row? _____

- _____ rows of _____ = _____

So, Mr. Hall's classroom has _____ chairs in all.

Complete each number sentence.

2. ▢▢▢▢▢▢

_____ row of _____ = _____

3. (array of 8 columns × 4 rows)

_____ rows of _____ = _____

4. (array of 7 columns × 3 rows)

_____ rows of _____ = _____

5. (array of 4 columns × 2 rows)

_____ rows of _____ = _____

6. (array of 6 columns × 5 rows)

_____ows of _____ = _____

7. (array of 8 columns × 4 rows)

_____ rows of _____ = _____

_____ growing corn in her garden. She plants 6 rows
_____ with 9 plants in each row. How many corn plants

_____

Meaning of Division: Equal Groups
Skill 5

Objective
To make equal groups to explore the meaning of division

Vocabulary
divide To separate into equal groups; the opposite operation of multiplication

Manipulatives
counters, MathBoard

COMMON ERROR

- Students may have trouble separating counters to find the number in each group.

- To correct this, encourage students to put one counter into each group and then put another counter into each group until no counters are left.

Learn the Math page IN19 Explain that the model in Example 1 shows dividing to find the number in each group. Have students use counters to create the model shown in the Steps 1–3. Ask: **How many counters are in each group?** 6 counters

Explain that the model in Example 2 shows dividing to find the number of equal groups. Tell students to place 18 counters on a sheet of paper for Step 1. In Steps 2 and 3, have them draw an outline around the counters to create groups of 9. Ask: **How many groups are there?** 2 groups **How is the model in Example 2 different from Example 1?** Possible answer: In Example 2, I know how many counters are in each group, and I need to find the number of equal groups.

In Example 1, I know the number of equal groups, and I need to find the number of counters in each group.

REASONING Encourage students to use 18 counters and model making as many groups of 3 as they can. Students should make 6 groups of 3 counters.

Do the Math page IN20 Discuss Exercise 1 with students. Ask: **How can you find the number of desks in each row?** Count out 24 counters. Make 4 equal groups by placing 1 counter in each group until all of the counters are used.

Assign Exercises 2–11 and monitor students' work.

Encourage students to use counters to model Problem 12. Ask: **Do you know the number of groups or the number of counters in each group?** the number of groups

Students who make more than 3 errors in Exercises 1–12 may benefit from the **Alternative Teaching Strategy**.

Alternative Teaching Strategy
Manipulatives and Materials: counters, paper plates

Have pairs of students use counters and paper plates to act out dividing to find the number in each group or the number of equal groups. Start with 24 counters. Have students divide the counters equally among 3 paper plates. Ask: **How many are in each group?** 8 in each group Have them record 3 groups with 8 in each group. Now have students decide how many plates they need to put the 24 counters into groups of 4. Ask: **How many paper plates are needed for the groups?** 6 plates Record 6 groups with 4 in each group. Repeat using other division facts.

Meaning of Division: Equal Groups
Skill **5**

Learn the Math

When you divide, you separate into equal groups.

Example 1 Divide to find the number in each group.

Kendra has 18 beads. She wants to make 3 bracelets, each with the same number of beads. How many beads will be on each bracelet?

Vocabulary

divide

Step 1	Step 2	Step 3
Use 18 counters to represent the beads.	Show 3 groups to represent the bracelets. Place 1 counter in each group.	Continue until all 18 counters are used. There are __6__ counters in each group.

So, there will be __6__ beads on 3 bracelets.

Example 2 Divide to find the number of equal groups.

Kendra decides she wants to put 9 beads on each bracelet. How many bracelets can she make?

Step 1	Step 2	Step 3
Use 18 counters to represent the beads.	Circle a group of 9 counters.	Continue circling groups of 9 until all 18 counters are in groups. There are __2__ groups of 9 counters.

So, Kendra can make __2__ bracelets.

REASONING If Kendra wants to put 3 beads on each bracelet, how many bracelets can she make? Explain your answer.

6 bracelets; Possible answer: you can make groups of 3 until all of the counters are in groups. There are 6 groups of 3 counters.

Response to Intervention • Tier 2 **IN19**

Do the Math

Skill **5**

1. Mr. Gomez wants to arrange 24 desks in his classroom into 4 equal rows. How many desks will be in each row?

- How many desks are there in all? __24__
- How many equal groups are there? __4__
- Use 24 counters. Make 4 equal groups.
- How many counters are in each group? __6__

So, there are __6__ desks in each row.

Remember
- When you divide, you separate into equal groups.
- Using counters can help you see how many items are in each group and how many equal groups you have.

Complete the table. Use counters to help.

	Counters	Number of Equal Groups	Number in Each Group
2.	16	2	__8__
3.	27	__3__	9
4.	10	5	__2__
5.	32	8	__4__
6.	21	__3__	7
7.	36	__9__	4
8.	9	3	__3__
9.	40	__8__	5
10.	24	__3__	8
11.	28	7	__4__

12. Lauren has 35 stickers. She puts an equal number of stickers on each of 7 pages of her sticker book. How many stickers are on each page?

5 stickers

IN20 Response to Intervention • Tier 2

Name _____

Learn the Math

When you divide, you separate into equal groups.

Vocabulary

divide

Example 1 Divide to find the number in each group.

Kendra has 18 beads. She wants to make 3 bracelets, each with the same number of beads. How many beads will be on each bracelet?

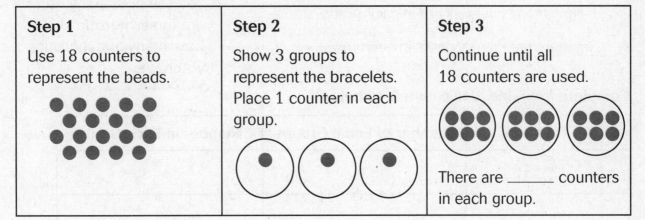

Step 1	Step 2	Step 3
Use 18 counters to represent the beads.	Show 3 groups to represent the bracelets. Place 1 counter in each group.	Continue until all 18 counters are used. There are _____ counters in each group.

So, there will be _____ beads on 3 bracelets.

Example 2 Divide to find the number of equal groups.

Kendra decides she wants to put 9 beads on each bracelet. How many bracelets can she make?

Step 1	Step 2	Step 3
Use 18 counters to represent the beads. 	Circle a group of 9 counters. 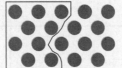	Continue circling groups of 9 until all 18 counters are in groups. 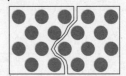 There are _____ groups of 9 counters.

So, Kendra can make _____ bracelets.

REASONING If Kendra wants to put 3 beads on each bracelet, how many bracelets can she make? Explain your answer.

_____

_____

1. Mr. Gomez wants to arrange 24 desks in his classroom into 4 equal rows. How many desks will be in each row?

   • How many desks are there in all? _____

   • How many equal groups are there? _____

   • Use 24 counters. Make 4 equal groups.

   • How many counters are in each group? _____

   So, there are _____ desks in each row.

> **Remember**
> • When you divide, you separate into equal groups.
> • Using counters can help you see how many items are in each group and how many equal groups you have.

Complete the table. Use counters to help.

	Counters	Number of Equal Groups	Number in Each Group
2.	16	2	_____
3.	27	_____	9
4.	10	5	_____
5.	32	8	_____
6.	21	_____	7
7.	36	_____	4
8.	9	3	_____
9.	40	_____	5
10.	24	_____	8
11.	28	7	_____

12. Lauren has 35 stickers. She puts an equal number of stickers on each of 7 pages of her sticker book. How many stickers are on each page?

_____

Meaning of Division: Arrays
Skill 6

Objective
To use arrays to explore the meaning of division

Vocabulary
array A set of objects or numbers arranged in equal rows and columns

Manipulatives
square tiles

COMMON ERROR

- Students may confuse the number of rows in an array with the number of tiles in a row.

- To correct this, relate arrays to equal groups. Explain that the number of rows in an array is the same as the number of equal groups and that the number of tiles in a row is the same as the number of items in an equal group.

Learn the Math page IN23 Guide students through Example 1. Discuss that objects form arrays when they are arranged in equal rows. Ask students to make the array using square tiles.

Direct students to Example 2. Explain that each row in the array represents an equal group. Ask: **How many tiles are there in all?** 18 tiles **How many tiles are in each row?** 6 tiles **How many equal rows are in the array?** 3 rows

REASONING Read and discuss the problem with students. Ask students to count out 72 tiles and model equal rows of 9. Students should model an array with 8 rows of 9 tiles.

Do the Math page IN24 Guide students through Exercise 1. Have them use square tiles to model the problem. Ask: **How many tiles do you use in all?** 20 tiles **How many tiles are in each row?** 4 tiles **How many equal rows are there?** 5 rows

Assign Exercises 2–7 and monitor students' work.

Discuss Problem 8. Instruct students to use square tiles to model the problem. Ask: **How can you use square tiles to model this problem?** Possible answer: count out 56 tiles. Make rows of 8 until all the tiles are used. There are 7 rows of 8 tiles.

Students who make more than 2 errors in Exercises 1–8 may benefit from the **Alternative Teaching Strategy**.

Alternative Teaching Strategy
Manipulatives: square tiles

Group students into pairs. Give each pair of students square tiles. Write *6 rows of ? in 30* on the board. Have each pair of students count out 30 tiles. Instruct them to begin an array by making a column with 6 tiles. Explain that this array has 6 rows of 1. Have students take turns adding one tile to each row until all the tiles have been used. Ask: **How many tiles are in each row?** 5 tiles

Repeat with other division facts.

Name _____

Learn the Math

You can use arrays to model division and find equal groups.

Vocabulary

array

Example 1

Yara has 28 coins in her coin collection. She puts them in rows of 7 to show her friends. How many rows of coins does she have?

Show the number of coins using an array.

Step 1	Step 2	Step 3
Count out 28 tiles. Make an array to find how many rows of 7 are in 28.	Make a row of 7 tiles.	Continue to make rows of 7 tiles until all 28 tiles have been used.
		There are ___4___ rows of tiles.

So, Yara has ___4___ rows with ___7___ coins in each row.

Example 2

Make an array to find how many rows of 6 are in 18.

There are ___6___ tiles in each row.

There are ___3___ equal rows.

So, there are ___3___ rows of 6 in 18.

REASONING Explain how to make an array to find how many rows of 9 you can make with 72 tiles.

Possible answer: make rows of 9 until all 72 tiles are used.

There are 8 rows. So, there are 8 rows of 9 in 72.

Response to Intervention • Tier 2 **IN23**

Do the Math

Skill **6**

1. Ms. Schmick plants 20 flowers in her garden. She plants 4 flowers in each row. How many rows of flowers does she have? Use tiles to make an array.

• How many flowers are there in all? ___20___

• How many flowers are in each row? ___4___

• How many rows of 4 are there? ___5___

• There are ___5___ rows of ___4___ in 20.

So, Ms. Schmick has ___5___ rows with ___4___ flowers in each row.

Remember
• Count out the total number of tiles first.
• Make equal rows until you have used all of the tiles.

Complete for each array.

2. ___12___ tiles in all
___4___ tiles in each row
___3___ equal rows

3. ___6___ tiles in all
___3___ tiles in each row
___2___ equal rows

4. ___27___ tiles in all
___9___ tiles in each row
___3___ equal rows

5. ___8___ tiles in all
___2___ tiles in each row
___4___ equal rows

6. ___21___ tiles in all
___7___ tiles in each row
___3___ equal rows

7. ___10___ tiles in all
___5___ tiles in each row
___2___ equal rows

8. Mr. Curtin plants 56 sunflowers in rows of 8. How many rows of 8 does he plant?
___7 rows___

IN24 Response to Intervention • Tier 2

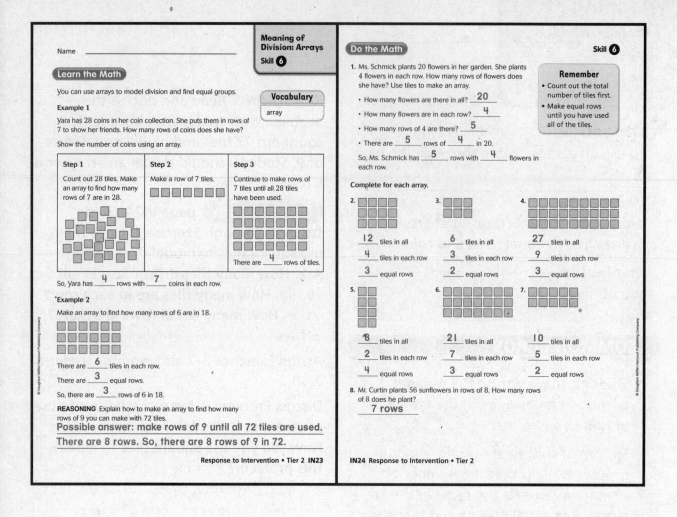

Name _____

Learn the Math

You can use arrays to model division and find equal groups.

Vocabulary

array

Example 1

Yara has 28 coins in her coin collection. She puts them in rows of 7 to show her friends. How many rows of coins does she have?

Show the number of coins using an array.

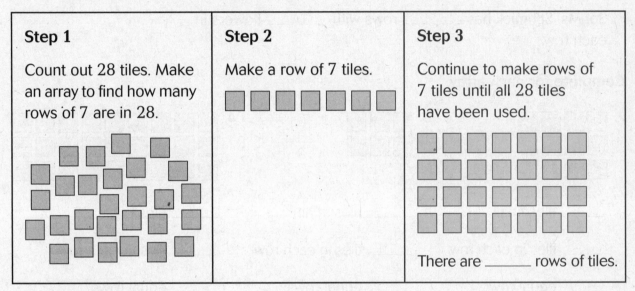

Step 1	Step 2	Step 3
Count out 28 tiles. Make an array to find how many rows of 7 are in 28.	Make a row of 7 tiles.	Continue to make rows of 7 tiles until all 28 tiles have been used.

There are _____ rows of tiles.

So, Yara has _____ rows with _____ coins in each row.

Example 2

Make an array to find how many rows of 6 are in 18.

There are _____ tiles in each row.

There are _____ equal rows.

So, there are _____ rows of 6 in 18.

REASONING Explain how to make an array to find how many rows of 9 you can make with 72 tiles.

_____

_____

1. Ms. Schmick plants 20 flowers in her garden. She plants 4 flowers in each row. How many rows of flowers does she have? Use tiles to make an array.

- How many flowers are there in all? _____

- How many flowers are in each row? _____

- How many rows of 4 are there? _____

- There are _____ rows of _____ in 20.

So, Ms. Schmick has _____ rows with _____ flowers in each row.

> **Remember**
> - Count out the total number of tiles first.
> - Make equal rows until you have used all of the tiles.

Complete for each array.

2.

_____ tiles in all

_____ tiles in each row

_____ equal rows

3.

_____ tiles in all

_____ tiles in each row

_____ equal rows

4.

_____ tiles in all

_____ tiles in each row

_____ equal rows

5.

_____ tiles in all

_____ tiles in each row

_____ equal rows

6.

_____ tiles in all

_____ tiles in each row

_____ equal rows

7.

_____ tiles in all

_____ tiles in each row

_____ equal rows

8. Mr. Curtin plants 56 sunflowers in rows of 8. How many rows of 8 does he plant?

_____

Use a Rule
Skill 7

Objective
To use a rule to complete a function table

COMMON ERROR

- Students may have difficulty seeing the relationship between the two rows in a function table.

- To correct this, draw a function table on the board that shows the relationship between the number of students and the number of feet they have. Discuss each column in the table. Show that the rule, *Multiply the number of students by 2*, applies to each column.

Learn the Math page IN27 Discuss Example 1 with the students. Read the pattern and a rule for the table aloud. Guide students to see that the rule applies to each column in the table. Ask: **How many batteries will be needed for 7 flashlights?** 21 **8 flashlights?** 24

Direct students to the table in Example 2. Read the pattern and a rule for the table aloud. Discuss that this rule uses division rather than multiplication.

REASONING Direct students to analyze the information in the table. Help them write a rule by identifying the relationship between the rows in the table. Ask: **One times what value equals $5?** $5 **Two times what value equals $10?** $5 **Three times**

what value equals $15? $5 Then have students use the rule to solve the problem. 4 × $5 = $20

Do the Math page IN28 Discuss Exercise 1 with students. Guide them to complete the pattern and a rule. Ask: **How many legs are on 3 spiders?** 24 legs

Assign Exercises 2–7 and monitor students' work.

Discuss Problem 8. Read the pattern aloud. Ask students to use the pattern to help them write a rule.

Students who make more than 2 errors in Exercises 1–8 may benefit from the **Alternative Teaching Strategy**.

Alternative Teaching Strategy
Materials: boxes of 8 crayons

Show one box of 8 crayons to the class. Ask for a volunteer to count the number of crayons in one box. Draw a table on the board as shown.

Boxes	1	2	3	4	5	6	7
Crayons	8						

Ask students to think of a way they can find the total number of crayons in 7 boxes.

Show students another box of 8 crayons. Then ask what number to write beneath the 2 in the table. 16 Repeat this for 3 and 4 boxes. 24, 32 Ask: **What is a pattern for the table?** Possible answer: the number of crayons equals the number of boxes times 8.

Have students use a rule to find the number of crayons in 5, 6, and 7 boxes. 40, 48, 56 Have a volunteer fill in the table and write a rule on the board. Possible answer: multiply the number of boxes by 8.

Learn the Math

The camping club is planning a trip. Each camper will need a flashlight. One flashlight uses 3 batteries. How many batteries are needed for 7 flashlights?

Example 1

Look for a pattern. Use a rule to complete the table.

Flashlights	1	2	3	4	5	6	7
Batteries	3	6	9	12	15	18	

Pattern: The number of batteries equals the number of flashlights times 3.

Rule: Multiply the number of flashlights by 3.

To find the number of batteries
needed for 7 flashlights, multiply 7 × 3. $7 \times 3 =$ __21__

So, __21__ batteries are needed for 7 flashlights.

Example 2

Look for a pattern. Use a rule to complete the table.

Number of batteries	4	8	12	16	20
Packs of batteries	1		3	4	

Pattern: The number of packs of batteries equals the number of batteries divided by 4.

Rule: Divide the number of batteries by 4.

How many packs will 8 batteries make? __2__ 20 batteries? __5__

REASONING Write a rule for the table. Find the cost of 4 packs of batteries.

Packs of batteries	1	2	3	4
Cost	$5	$10	$15	

Possible answer: multiply the number of packs of batteries by $5. 4 × $5 = $20. The cost of 4 packs is $20.

Do the Math

Skill 7

1. Look for a pattern. Use a rule to complete the table.

Spiders	1	2	3	4	5
Legs	8	16		32	40

Remember
Look for a relationship between the two rows of numbers in the table.

- Pattern: The number of legs equals the number of spiders __times 8__
- Rule: multiply the number of spiders by __8__
- $3 \times 8 =$ __24__

So, there __24__ legs on 3 spiders.

Complete each table.

2.
Legs	8	12	16	20	24
Dogs	2	3	4	5	6

Rule: Divide the number of legs by 4.

3.
Cars	1	2	3	4	5
Tires	4	8	12	16	20

Rule: Multiply the number of cars by 4.

4.
Students	1	2	3	4
Shoes	2	4	6	8

Rule: Multiply the number of students by 2.

5.
Pencils	8	24	32	40	48
Boxes	1	3	4	5	6

Rule: Divide the number of pencils by 8.

6.
Pennies	15	20	25	30	35
Nickels	3	4	5	6	7

Rule: Divide the number of pennies by 5.

7.
Teams	4	5	6	7	8
Players	24	30	36	42	48

Rule: Multiply the number of teams by 6.

8. Write a rule for the table and find the number of shoes needed for 4 horses.

Pattern: The number of shoes equals the number of horses times 4.

Horses	1	2	3	4
Shoes	4	8	12	

Possible answer: multiply the number of horses by 4. 4 × 4 = 16. For 4 horses, 16 shoes are needed.

Name _____

Learn the Math

The camping club is planning a trip. Each camper will need a flashlight. One flashlight uses 3 batteries. How many batteries are needed for 7 flashlights?

Example 1

Look for a pattern. Use a rule to complete the table.

Flashlights	1	2	3	4	5	6	7
Batteries	3	6	9	12	15	18	⬜

Pattern: The number of batteries equals the number of flashlights times 3.

Rule: Multiply the number of flashlights by 3.

To find the number of batteries needed for 7 flashlights, multiply 7×3.

$7 \times 3 =$ _____

So, _____ batteries are needed for 7 flashlights.

Example 2

Look for a pattern. Use a rule to complete the table.

Number of batteries	4	8	12	16	20
Packs of batteries	1	⬜	3	4	⬜

Pattern: The number of packs of batteries equals the number of batteries divided by 4.

Rule: Divide the number of batteries by 4.

How many packs will 8 batteries make? _____ 20 batteries? _____

REASONING Write a rule for the table. Find the cost of 4 packs of batteries.

Packs of batteries	1	2	3	4
Cost	$5	$10	$15	⬜

_____

_____

1. Look for a pattern. Use a rule to complete the table.

Spiders	1	2	3	4	5
Legs	8	16	⬜	32	40

Remember
Look for a relationship between the two rows of numbers in the table.

- Pattern: The number of legs equals the number of spiders _____.

- Rule: multiply the number of spiders by _____.

- $3 \times 8 =$ _____

So, there _____ legs on 3 spiders.

Complete each table.

2.

Legs	8	12	16	20	24
Dogs	2	3	___	5	6

Rule: Divide the number of legs by 4.

3.

Cars	1	2	3	4	5
Tires	4	8	___	___	20

Rule: Multiply the number of cars by 4.

4.

Students	1	2	3	4
Shoes		2	___	6	___

Rule: Multiply the number of students by 2.

5.

Pencils	8	24	32	40	48
Boxes	1	3	___	___	6

Rule: Divide the number of pencils by 8.

6.

Pennies	15	20	25	30	35
Nickels	3	4	5	___	___

Rule: Divide the number of pennies by 5.

7.

Teams	4	5	6	7	8
Players	24	30	___	42	___

Rule: Multiply the number of teams by 6.

8. Write a rule for the table and find the number of shoes needed for 4 horses.

Pattern: The number of shoes equals the number of horses times 4.

Horses	1	2	3	4
Shoes	4	8	12	⬜

Objective
To choose the operation to solve problems

Vocabulary
addition The process of finding the total number of items when two or more groups of items are joined

subtraction The process of finding how many are left when a number of items are taken away from a group of items; the process of finding the difference when two groups are compared

multiplication The process of finding the total number of items in two or more equal groups

division The process of sharing a number of items to find how many equal groups can be made or how many items will be in a group

COMMON ERROR

- Students may have difficulty choosing the appropriate operation to solve a word problem.

- To correct this, have students describe the action taking place in the problem, or encourage them to draw pictures or act out the problem using the given numbers. Remind them to determine what the problem is asking. Have them explain the problem in their own words before they choose the operation.

Learn the Math page IN31 Read the first example with students. Ask: **What do you need to find?** the number of shells Lauren and Erika found in all **What information do you need to use?** the number of shells Lauren found, 16, and the number of shells Erika found, 12 **How will you use the information?** Add to join the groups. **How many shells did the girls find in all?** 28 shells

Repeat this questioning process for the subtraction, multiplication, and division examples.

REASONING Discuss the problem with students. Ask: **What operation should you choose? Why?** multiplication; possible answer: because the problem involves joining equal amounts

Do the Math page IN32 Guide students through Exercise 1. Ask: **What do you need to find?** the number of shells Jacob found in all

Assign Exercises 2–8 and monitor students' work.

Students who make more than 2 errors in Exercises 1–8 may benefit from the **Alternative Teaching Strategy**.

Alternative Teaching Strategy
Have students practice choosing the operation in a variety of problems. The following questions are only parts of word problems. Read each question and have students choose the operation that would help answer the question. **How many are in each group?** division **How many are there in all?** addition or multiplication **How much more does Tim have than Rao?** subtraction **How many apples are in 3 baskets?** addition or multiplication **How many equal groups are there?** division Continue with similar questions.

Name _____

Learn the Math

Lauren and Erika spent a day at the beach looking for shells.

Sometimes, you need to decide which operation to use to solve a problem.

Add to join groups of different sizes.	Subtract to find the number left or to compare amounts.
Lauren found 16 shells and Erika found 12. How many shells did they find in all?	Lauren found 16 shells and Erika found 12. How many more shells did Lauren find than Erika?
16 ← Lauren's shells +12 ← Erika's shells **28** ← total number of shells	16 ← Lauren's shells −12 ← Erika's shells **4** ← how many more shells
Multiply to join equal amounts.	**Divide to separate into equal groups or to find the number in each group.**
The beach store sells shells for $3 each. What is the cost of 5 shells?	Lauren and Erika divide their 28 shells into 4 equal groups. How many shells are in each group?
5 × $3 = **$15** ↑ ↑ ↑ number of shells / cost of one shell / total cost	28 ÷ 4 = **7** ↑ ↑ ↑ number of shells / number of groups / shells in each group

REASONING What's the error? Lauren said that to find the cost of 9 shells you divide 9 by $3. Is she correct? Explain.

No; possible answer: to find the cost of

9 shells, you multiply. 9 × $3 = $27

Response to Intervention • Tier 2 **IN31**

---

1. Jacob found 9 shells in the morning and 15 in the afternoon. How many shells did he find in all?
   • What operation do you use? **addition**
   • Write a number sentence. 9 (+) 15 = **24**
   So, Jacob found **24** shells in all.

Remember
• Add to join groups of different sizes.
• Subtract to find the number left or to compare amounts.
• Multiply to join equal amounts.
• Divide to separate into equal groups or to find the number in each group.

Write +, −, ×, or ÷ to complete the number sentence.

2. Kyle has 30 baseball cards. He divides them into 6 equal groups. How many cards are in each group?
   30 (÷) 6 = 5 **5** cards in each group

3. There are 8 teams with 9 students on each team. How many students are there in all?
   8 (×) 9 = 72 **72** students

4. Edna had 22 markers. She gave 6 away. How many markers does she have left?
   22 (−) 6 = 16 **16** markers

5. Posters are sold for $7 in the school library. What is the cost of 3 posters?
   3 (×) $7 = $21 **$21** for 3 posters

6. There are 12 girls and 11 boys in Mrs. Reed's class. How many students are there in all?
   12 (+) 11 = 23 **23** students

7. There are 15 boys and 10 girls in Mr. Martin's class. How many more boys are there than girls?
   15 (−) 10 = 5 **5** more boys

8. Sarah shares 24 cookies with friends. She gives each friend 3 cookies. With how many friends does she share the cookies?
   24 (÷) 3 = 8 **8** friends

IN32 Response to Intervention • Tier 2

Name _____

Learn the Math

Lauren and Erika spent a day at the beach looking for shells.

Sometimes, you need to decide which operation to use to solve a problem.

Vocabulary

addition
subtraction
multiplication
division

Add to join groups of different sizes.
 	
Lauren found 16 shells and Erika found 12. How many shells did they find in all?
 	
  16 ← Lauren's shells
+12 ← Erika's shells
 ☐ ← total number of shells
	Subtract to find the number left or to compare amounts.
	
	Lauren found 16 shells and Erika found 12. How many more shells did Lauren find than Erika?
	
	  16 ← Lauren's shells
	−12 ← Erika's shells
	 ☐ ← how many more shells

Multiply to join equal amounts.
 	
The beach store sells shells for \$3 each. What is the cost of 5 shells?
 	
  5   ×   \$3   = _____
  ↑   ↑   ↑
number   cost of   total cost
of shells   one shell
	Divide to separate into equal groups or to find the number in each group.
	
	Lauren and Erika divide their 28 shells into 4 equal groups. How many shells are in each group?
	
	  28 ÷ 4 = _____
	  ↑ ↑ ↑
	number number shells in
	of shells of groups each group

REASONING What's the error? Lauren said that to find the cost of 9 shells you divide 9 by \$3. Is she correct? Explain.

_____

_____

1. Jacob found 9 shells in the morning and 15 in the afternoon. How many shells did he find in all?

   • What operation do you use? _____

   • Write a number sentence. 9 ◯ 15 = _____

   So, Jacob found _____ shells in all.

Remember
• Add to join groups of different sizes.
• Subtract to find the number left or to compare amounts.
• Multiply to join equal amounts.
• Divide to separate into equal groups or to find the number in each group.

Write +, −, ×, or ÷ to complete the number sentence.

2. Kyle has 30 baseball cards. He divides them into 6 equal groups. How many cards are in each group?

   30 ◯ 6 = 5   _____ cards in each group

3. There are 8 teams with 9 students on each team. How many students are there in all?

   8 ◯ 9 = 72   _____ students

4. Edna had 22 markers. She gave 6 away. How many markers does she have left?

   22 ◯ 6 = 16   _____ markers

5. Posters are sold for $7 in the school library. What is the cost of 3 posters?

   3 ◯ $7 = $21   _____ for 3 posters

6. There are 12 girls and 11 boys in Mrs. Reed's class. How many students are there in all?

   12 ◯ 11 = 23   _____ students

7. There are 15 boys and 10 girls in Mr. Martin's class. How many more boys are there than girls?

   15 ◯ 10 = 5   _____ more boys

8. Sarah shares 24 cookies with friends. She gives each friend 3 cookies. With how many friends does she share the cookies?

   24 ◯ 3 = 8   _____ friends

Objective
To practice multiplication facts through 9×9

Manipulatives and Materials
counters, multiplication table, number lines (see *Teacher Resources*)

COMMON ERROR

- When using a multiplication table, students may confuse the terms *row* and *column*.

- To correct this, write *row* and *column* on the left and top sides of the multiplication table, respectively.

Learn the Math page IN35 Review the problem with students. Explain that this problem can be solved using different strategies.

Guide students through using a multiplication table. Demonstrate on a large multiplication table how row 3 and column 4 meet at 12.

Discuss using a number line. Have students trace the jumps on the number line as they skip count by fours 3 times. Ask: **On what number do you stop?** 12

Direct students to the model using counters. Have students make 3 groups of 4 using counters. Ask: **How many groups of 4 do you have?** 3 groups Ask: **How many counters are there in all?** 12 counters

Remind students that there are other strategies they can use to find products.

The three models shown on page IN35 are only some of the strategies they have learned.

REASONING Discuss the question with students. Encourage them to find the answer using different strategies. Ask for student volunteers to show how they found the product.

Do the Math page IN36 Review Exercise 1 with students. Ask: **How can you use counters to find the product?** First, find the number of equal groups. Then, find the number of counters in each group. **Guide students to solve the problem.**

Assign Exercises 2–24 and monitor students' work.

Discuss Problem 25. Have students model the problem using counters. Ask: **How many equal groups do you make?** 6 equal groups **How many counters do you put in each group?** 4 counters **How many counters are there in all?** 24 counters

Students who make more than 7 errors in Exercises 1–25 may benefit from the **Alternative Teaching Strategy**.

Alternative Teaching Strategy
Manipulatives: square tiles

Have students use arrays to model multiplication facts. Write 5×6 on the board. Have students make an array using 5 rows of 6 tiles. Ask: **What is 5×6?** 30

Next write 4×8. Ask: **How many rows will you make?** 4 rows **How many tiles will you have in each row?** 8 tiles Direct students to make the array. Ask: **What is 4×8?** 32 Repeat with similar problems.

Name _____

Learn the Math

Jacob washes 4 cars per hour at a car wash. How many cars does Jacob wash in 3 hours?

$3 \times 4 =$ ▢

You can use multiplication strategies to help solve the problem.

Use a multiplication table.
Find the product for 3×4 where row 3 and column 4 meet.

$3 \times 4 =$ __12__

What do you notice about all of the numbers in column 4?

__Possible answer: none__
__of the numbers are odd.__

Use a number line.
Begin at 0. Draw jumps on the number line to skip count by fours.

Make __3__ jumps of __4__ spaces each.

$3 \times 4 =$ __12__

Use counters.
Show 3 groups of 4.
Skip count by fours.

3 groups of 4 = __12__

$3 \times 4 =$ __12__

4   8   12

So, Jacob washes __12__ cars in 3 hours.

REASONING How many cars can Jacob wash if he works for 5 hours? Explain how you can use a strategy to find the product.

__20 cars; possible answer: I can use a number line__

__and make 5 jumps of 4 spaces each.__

Response to Intervention • Tier 2 **IN35**

Do the Math

1. Julie has 5 boxes with 6 pencils in each box. How many pencils does Julie have in all?

- How many groups of pencils are there? __5__
- How many pencils are in each group? __6__
- Make __5__ groups of __6__ counters.

> **Remember**
> You can use different strategies, such as *use a multiplication table*, *use a number line*, or *use counters*, to find a product.

- $5 \times 6 =$ __30__

So, Julie has __30__ pencils in all.

Find the product.

2.

$2 \times 7 =$ __14__

3.

$5 \times 3 =$ __15__

4. $7 \times 5 =$ __35__	5. $9 \times 1 =$ __9__	6. $7 \times 0 =$ __0__
7. __28__ $= 4 \times 7$	8. __4__ $= 2 \times 2$	9. $6 \times 9 =$ __54__
10. $5 \times 8 =$ __40__	11. $6 \times 4 =$ __24__	12. __36__ $= 9 \times 4$
13. $7 \times 3 =$ __21__	14. $8 \times 3 =$ __24__	15. __56__ $= 8 \times 7$
16. __2__ $= 2 \times 1$	17. __0__ $= 9 \times 0$	18. $6 \times 8 =$ __48__
19. $3 \times 9 =$ __27__	20. __42__ $= 7 \times 6$	21. $1 \times 8 =$ __8__
22. __16__ $= 4 \times 4$	23. $9 \times 2 =$ __18__	24. __20__ $= 5 \times 4$

25. Yolanda gives 4 carrots each to 6 of her friends at snacktime. How many carrots does Yolanda give in all? __24 carrots__

IN36 Response to Intervention • Tier 2

Name _____

Learn the Math

Jacob washes 4 cars per hour at a car wash. How many cars does Jacob wash in 3 hours?

$3 \times 4 =$ ▢

You can use multiplication strategies to help solve the problem.

Use a multiplication table.

Find the product for 3×4 where row 3 and column 4 meet.

$3 \times 4 =$ _____

What do you notice about all of the numbers in column 4?

_____

_____

×	0	1	2	3	4	5	6	7	8	9
0	0	0	0	0	0	0	0	0	0	0
1	0	1	2	3	4	5	6	7	8	9
2	0	2	4	6	8	10	12	14	16	18
3	0	3	6	9	12	15	18	21	24	27
4	0	4	8	12	16	20	24	28	32	36
5	0	5	10	15	20	25	30	35	40	45
6	0	6	12	18	24	30	36	42	48	54
7	0	7	14	21	28	35	42	49	56	63
8	0	8	16	24	32	40	48	56	64	72
9	0	9	18	27	36	45	54	63	72	81

Use a number line.

Begin at 0. Draw jumps on the number line to skip count by fours.

Make _____ jumps of _____ spaces each.

$3 \times 4 =$ _____

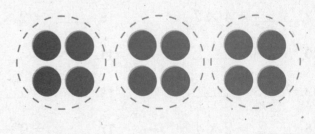

0 1 2 3 4 5 6 7 8 9 10 11 12 13 14 15

Use counters.

Show 3 groups of 4.
Skip count by fours.

3 groups of 4 = _____

$3 \times 4 =$ _____

_____   _____   _____

So, Jacob washes _____ cars in 3 hours.

REASONING How many cars can Jacob wash if he works for 5 hours? Explain how you can use a strategy to find the product.

_____

_____

1. Julie has 5 boxes with 6 pencils in each box.
How many pencils does Julie have in all?

• How many groups of pencils are there? _____

• How many pencils are in each group? _____

• Make _____ groups of _____ counters.

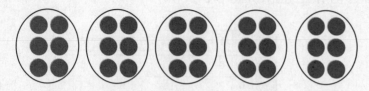

• $5 \times 6 =$ _____

So, Julie has _____ pencils in all.

> **Remember**
> You can use different strategies, such as *use a multiplication table*, *use a number line*, or *use counters*, to find a product.

Find the product.

2.

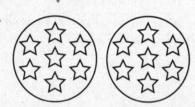

$2 \times 7 =$ _____

3.

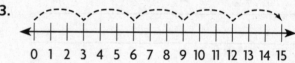

$$5 \times 3 = \underline{\hspace{1cm}}$$

4. $7 \times 5 =$ _____

5. $9 \times 1 =$ _____

6. $7 \times 0 =$ _____

7. _____ $= 4 \times 7$

8. _____ $= 2 \times 2$

9. $6 \times 9 =$ _____

10. $5 \times 8 =$ _____

11. $6 \times 4 =$ _____

12. _____ $= 9 \times 4$

13. $7 \times 3 =$ _____

14. $8 \times 3 =$ _____

15. _____ $= 8 \times 7$

16. _____ $= 2 \times 1$

17. _____ $= 9 \times 0$

18. $6 \times 8 =$ _____

19. $3 \times 9 =$ _____

20. _____ $= 7 \times 6$

21. $1 \times 8 =$ _____

22. _____ $= 4 \times 4$

23. $9 \times 2 =$ _____

24. _____ $= 5 \times 4$

25. Yolanda gives 4 carrots each to 6 of her friends at snacktime.
How many carrots does Yolanda give in all? _____

Regroup Through Thousands
Skill 10

Objective
To understand regrouping of hundreds, tens, and ones

Vocabulary
regroup To exchange amounts of equal value to rename a number

Manipulatives
base-ten blocks

COMMON ERROR

- Students may regroup only one time even though there are enough hundreds, tens, or ones to regroup again.

- To correct this, have students model regrouping with base-ten blocks. Remind them to count the number of hundreds, tens, or ones before writing the number.

Learn the Math page IN39 Discuss Example 1 with students. Guide them through Steps 1–3. Instruct students to use base-ten blocks to model the number as shown in Step 1. Have them trade 10 ones for 1 ten as shown in Step 2. Elicit that 4 tens 16 ones and 5 tens 6 ones are different ways to write the same number.

Discuss Example 2. Have students use base-ten blocks to model Steps 1–3. Assist students as they trade 10 ones for 1 ten as shown in Step 2 and then as they trade 20 tens for 2 hundreds as shown in Step 3.

Review that you can regroup 10 ones as 1 ten, 10 tens as 1 hundred, and 10 hundreds as 1 thousand.

REASONING Discuss the question with students. Show students how modeling

6 tens 17 ones, 7 tens 6 ones, and 67 with base-ten blocks can help them determine which number is greatest.

Do the Math page IN40 Discuss Exercise 1 with students. Provide base-ten blocks to help students solve the problem. Ask: **How can you use base-ten blocks to find the number of cards in all?** I can show 6 tens 18 ones with base-ten blocks and then regroup 10 ones as 1 ten.

Assign Exercises 2–15 and monitor students' work.

Discuss Problem 16. Instruct students to model the problem using base-ten blocks. Ask: **Do you have enough ones to regroup?** yes Assist students as they trade 10 ones for 1 ten. Ask: **How many tens and ones do you have now?** 5 tens 6 ones **How many flowers does Greg have in all?** 56 flowers

Students who make more than 4 errors in Exercises 1–16 may benefit from the **Alternative Teaching Strategy**.

Alternative Teaching Strategy
Have students use place value to regroup. Write 9 hundreds 9 tens 10 ones on the board. Ask: **Do you have enough ones to regroup?** yes **How many ones are left after you regroup?** 0 ones Write the number on the board as 9 hundreds 10 tens. Say: **You can regroup 10 tens as 1 hundred and 10 hundreds as 1 thousand.** Ask: **Do you have enough tens to regroup?** yes **How many tens are left after you regroup?** 0 tens Write 10 hundreds on the board. Ask: **Do you have enough hundreds to regroup?** yes **How many hundreds are left after you regroup?** 0 hundreds Write 1 thousand on the board. Repeat with similar examples.

Regroup Through Thousands
Skill 10

Learn the Math

You can regroup to write a number in different ways.

Example 1
Regroup. Then rewrite the number as tens and ones.

4 tens 16 ones

Vocabulary

regroup

Step 1	Step 2	Step 3
Show 4 tens 16 ones using base-ten blocks.	Regroup 10 ones as 1 ten.	Rewrite the number as tens and ones.
		5 tens 6 ones

So, 4 tens 16 ones = __5__ tens __6__ ones.

Example 2
Regroup. Then rewrite the number as hundreds.

19 tens 10 ones

Step 1	Step 2	Step 3
Show 19 tens 10 ones using base-ten blocks.	Regroup 10 ones as 1 ten.	Regroup 20 tens as 2 hundreds.

So, 19 tens 10 ones = __2__ hundreds.

REASONING Which is the greatest number? Explain.

6 tens 17 ones   7 tens 6 ones   67

6 tens 17 ones; possible answer: 6 tens 17 ones = 77 and 7 tens 6 ones = 76. The greatest number of 77, 76, and 67 is 77.

Response to Intervention • Tier 2 **IN39**

Do the Math

Skill 10

1. Leo has 6 packs of baseball cards. Each pack has 10 cards. He has 18 cards that are not in packs. How many cards does Leo have in all?

You can regroup to find the number of cards.

- Write how many baseball cards Leo has as tens and ones.
  6 tens __18__ ones
- 18 ones = __1__ ten 8 ones
- 6 tens 18 ones = __7__ tens 8 ones
  So, Leo has __78__ baseball cards in all.

Remember
- Regroup 10 ones as 1 ten.
- Regroup 10 tens as 1 hundred.
- Regroup 10 hundreds as 1 thousand.

Regroup. Write the missing numbers.

2.
9 tens 10 ones = __1__ hundred

3.
10 hundreds = __1__ thousand

4. 30 tens = __3__ hundreds

5. __4__ tens 13 ones = 5 tens 3 ones

6. 40 hundreds = __4__ thousands

7. 40 tens = __4__ hundreds

8. 18 tens 20 ones = __2__ hundreds

9. 20 hundreds = __2__ thousands

10. __2__ tens 14 ones = 3 tens 4 ones

11. 3 tens 17 ones = __4__ tens 7 ones

12. 80 tens = __8__ hundreds

13. 8 tens 20 ones = __1__ hundred

14. 1 hundred 9 tens 10 ones = __2__ hundreds

15. 10 tens = __1__ hundred

16. Greg puts flowers in 4 vases. Each vase has 10 flowers. He has 16 flowers left over. How many flowers does Greg have in all?
4 tens 16 ones = 5 tens 6 ones; 56 flowers

IN40 Response to Intervention • Tier 2

Name _____

Learn the Math

You can regroup to write a number in different ways.

Vocabulary

regroup

Example 1
Regroup. Then rewrite the number as tens and ones.

4 tens 16 ones

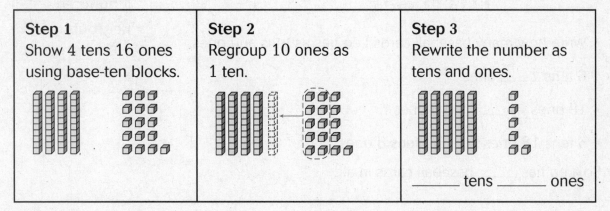

Step 1
Show 4 tens 16 ones using base-ten blocks.

Step 2
Regroup 10 ones as 1 ten.

Step 3
Rewrite the number as tens and ones.

_____ tens _____ ones

So, 4 tens 16 ones = _____ tens _____ ones.

Example 2
Regroup. Then rewrite the number as hundreds.

19 tens 10 ones

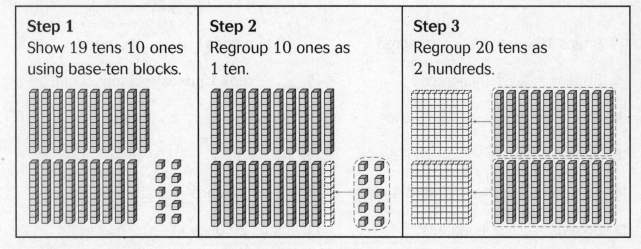

Step 1
Show 19 tens 10 ones using base-ten blocks.

Step 2
Regroup 10 ones as 1 ten.

Step 3
Regroup 20 tens as 2 hundreds.

So, 19 tens 10 ones = _____ hundreds.

REASONING Which is the greatest number? Explain.

6 tens 17 ones   7 tens 6 ones   67

_____

_____

1. Leo has 6 packs of baseball cards. Each pack has 10 cards. He has 18 cards that are not in packs. How many cards does Leo have in all?

   You can regroup to find the number of cards.

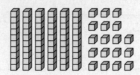

   Remember
   - Regroup 10 ones as 1 ten.
   - Regroup 10 tens as 1 hundred.
   - Regroup 10 hundreds as 1 thousand.

   • Write how many baseball cards Leo has as tens and ones.

   6 tens _____ ones

   • 18 ones = _____ ten 8 ones

   • 6 tens 18 ones = _____ tens 8 ones

   So, Leo has _____ baseball cards in all.

Regroup. Write the missing numbers.

2.

   9 tens 10 ones = _____ hundred

3.

   10 hundreds = _____ thousand

4. 30 tens = _____ hundreds

5. _____ tens 13 ones = 5 tens 3 ones

6. 40 hundreds = _____ thousands

7. 40 tens = _____ hundreds

8. 18 tens 20 ones = _____ hundreds

9. 20 hundreds = _____ thousands

10. _____ tens 14 ones = 3 tens 4 ones

11. 3 tens 17 ones = _____ tens 7 ones

12. 80 tens = _____ hundreds

13. 8 tens 20 ones = _____ hundred

14. 1 hundred 9 tens 10 ones = _____ hundreds

15. 10 tens = _____ hundred

16. Greg puts flowers in 4 vases. Each vase has 10 flowers. He has 16 flowers left over. How many flowers does Greg have in all?

Multiples of 10, 100, and 1,000
Skill 11

Objective
To use number lines or patterns and mental math to multiply multiples of 10, 100, and 1,000

Vocabulary
multiple A number that is the product of two counting numbers

COMMON ERROR

- Students may not write the correct number of zeros in the final product when a zero is in the product of the basic fact.

- To correct this, have students use patterns and underline the zeros in the patterns when multiplying multiples of 10, 100, and 1,000.

Learn the Math page IN43 Discuss the first number line in Example 1 with students. Have them skip count aloud as they identify the basic fact. Relate skip counting on a number line to repeated addition. Have students trace the jumps and identify the product for each of the next three number lines.

For Part A in Example 2, have students identify the number of zeros in the second factor and relate that number to the number of zeros in the product. Next discuss that in Part B, the number of zeros in the second factor is one fewer than the number of zeros in the product. Ask for a student volunteer to explain why. Possible answer: the basic fact has a zero in the ones place.

REASONING Ask: How can you tell how many zeros to include in the product of 4 × 5,000? Possible answer: there are 3 zeros in 5,000 and the product of the basic fact, 4 × 5 = 20, has 1 zero. So, the product has 4 zeros.

Do the Math page IN44 Discuss Exercise 1 with students. Guide them through finding the products on the number lines.

Assign Exercises 2–10 and monitor students' work.

Discuss Problem 11 with students. Ask: **How can you find the number of packs of stickers that Mr. Allen buys?** Possible answer: I can multiply 6 and 3,000. **How many packs of stickers does he buy?** 18,000 Students who make more than 3 errors in Exercises 1–11 may benefit from the **Alternative Teaching Strategy**.

Alternative Teaching Strategy
Manipulatives and Materials: square tiles, 1-inch grid paper (see *Teacher Resources*)

Give each pair of students a sheet of grid paper and 3 square tiles. Write 4 × 4,000 = on the board. Have each pair of students copy the problem onto their grid paper placing each digit within one square of the grid paper. Ask them to use the tiles to cover each zero in the factor 4,000 until only the basic fact is showing. 4 × 4 Have students find the product of the basic fact. 4 × 4 = 16 Next, have each pair of students count the number of tiles they used to cover the zeros. 3 Tell them that the number of tiles they used will be the number of zeros to include in the product of 4 × 4,000. 16,000 Repeat with similar problems.

© Houghton Mifflin Harcourt Publishing Company

Name _____

Learn the Math

You can use a number line or patterns and mental math to multiply multiples of 10, 100, and 1,000.

Vocabulary

multiple

Example 1 Use a number line.

Find $7 \times 2,000$.

Think of multiplication as repeated addition.

| 0 | 2 | 4 | 6 | 8 | 10 | 12 | 14 |

$7 \times 2 = 14$ ← basic fact

| 0 | 20 | 40 | 60 | 80 | 100 | 120 | 140 |

$7 \times 20 = \underline{140}$

| 0 | 200 | 400 | 600 | 800 | 1,000 | 1,200 | 1,400 |

$7 \times 200 = \underline{1,400}$

| 0 | 2,000 | 4,000 | 6,000 | 8,000 | 10,000 | 12,000 | 14,000 |

$7 \times 2,000 = \underline{14,000}$

So, $7 \times 2,000 = \underline{14,000}$.

Example 2 Use patterns and mental math.

A. Basic fact

$4 \times 3 = 12$ ← basic fact
$4 \times 30 = 120$
$4 \times 300 = \underline{1,200}$
$4 \times 3,000 = \underline{12,000}$

B. Basic fact with a zero

$6 \times 5 = 30$ ← basic fact
$6 \times 50 = 300$
$6 \times 500 = \underline{3,000}$
$6 \times 5,000 = \underline{30,000}$

REASONING How many zeros does the product of $4 \times 5,000$ have?
Write the product. Explain how you know.

4; 20,000; possible answer: 5,000 has 3 zeros, and the basic fact $4 \times 5 = 20$ has 1 zero. So, the product has 4 zeros.

Do the Math

1. Use a number line to find $2 \times 9,000$.

| 0 | 9 | 18 |

$2 \times 9 = \underline{18}$

| 0 | 90 | 180 |

$2 \times 90 = \underline{180}$

| 0 | 900 | 1,800 |

$2 \times 900 = \underline{1,800}$

| 0 | 9,000 | 18,000 |

$2 \times 9,000 = \underline{18,000}$

Remember

The number of zeros in the product increases as the number of zeros in a factor increases.

Use patterns and mental math to find the product.

2. $3 \times 5 = 15$ ← basic fact
$3 \times 50 = 150$
$3 \times 500 = \underline{1,500}$
$3 \times 5,000 = \underline{15,000}$

3. $8 \times 9 = 72$ ← basic fact
$8 \times 90 = 720$
$8 \times 900 = \underline{7,200}$
$8 \times 9,000 = \underline{72,000}$

4. $5 \times 7 = 35$ ← basic fact
$5 \times 70 = 350$
$5 \times 700 = \underline{3,500}$
$5 \times 7,000 = \underline{35,000}$

Find the product.

5. $9 \times 40 = \underline{360}$
$9 \times 400 = \underline{3,600}$
$9 \times 4,000 = \underline{36,000}$

6. $6 \times 20 = \underline{120}$
$6 \times 200 = \underline{1,200}$
$6 \times 2,000 = \underline{12,000}$

7. $4 \times 80 = \underline{320}$
$4 \times 800 = \underline{3,200}$
$4 \times 8,000 = \underline{32,000}$

8. $5 \times 10 = \underline{50}$
$5 \times 100 = \underline{500}$
$5 \times 1,000 = \underline{5,000}$

9. $8 \times 60 = \underline{480}$
$8 \times 600 = \underline{4,800}$
$8 \times 6,000 = \underline{48,000}$

10. $7 \times 90 = \underline{630}$
$7 \times 900 = \underline{6,300}$
$7 \times 9,000 = \underline{63,000}$

11. Mr. Allen buys 3,000 boxes of stickers for his store. Each box contains 6 packs of stickers. How many packs of stickers does Mr. Allen buy?

18,000 packs of stickers

Name _____

Learn the Math

You can use a number line or patterns and mental math to multiply multiples of 10, 100, and 1,000.

Example 1 Use a number line.

Find $7 \times 2,000$.
Think of multiplication as repeated addition.

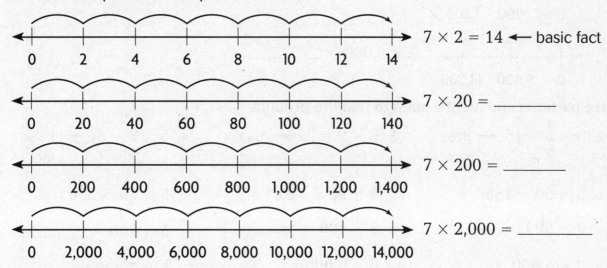

$7 \times 2 = 14$ ← basic fact

$7 \times 20 =$ _____

$7 \times 200 =$ _____

$7 \times 2,000 =$ _____

So, $7 \times 2,000 =$ _____.

Example 2 Use patterns and mental math.

A. Basic fact

$4 \times 3 = 12$ ← basic fact

$4 \times 30 = 120$

$4 \times 300 =$ _____

$4 \times 3,000 =$ _____

B. Basic fact with a zero

$6 \times 5 = 30$ ← basic fact

$6 \times 50 = 300$

$6 \times 500 =$ _____

$6 \times 5,000 =$ _____

REASONING How many zeros does the product of $4 \times 5,000$ have?
Write the product. Explain how you know.

_____

_____

© Houghton Mifflin Harcourt Publishing Company

1. Use a number line to find $2 \times 9,000$.

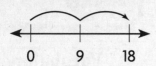 $2 \times 9 = $ _____

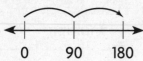 $2 \times 90 = $ _____

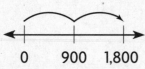 $2 \times 900 = $ _____

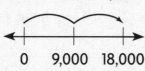 $2 \times 9,000 = $ _____

> **Remember**
> The number of zeros in the product increases as the number of zeros in a factor increases.

Use patterns and mental math to find the product.

2. $3 \times 5 = 15 \leftarrow$ basic
                          fact

   $3 \times 50 = 150$

   $3 \times 500 = $ _____

   $3 \times 5,000 = $ _____

3. $8 \times 9 = 72 \leftarrow$ basic
                          fact

   $8 \times 90 = 720$

   $8 \times 900 = $ _____

   $8 \times 9,000 = $ _____

4. $5 \times 7 = 35 \leftarrow$ basic
                          fact

   $5 \times 70 = 350$

   $5 \times 700 = $ _____

   $5 \times 7,000 = $ _____

Find the product.

5. $9 \times 40 = $ _____

   $9 \times 400 = $ _____

   $9 \times 4,000 = $ _____

6. $6 \times 20 = $ _____

   $6 \times 200 = $ _____

   $6 \times 2,000 = $ _____

7. $4 \times 80 = $ _____

   $4 \times 800 = $ _____

   $4 \times 8,000 = $ _____

8. $5 \times 10 = $ _____

   $5 \times 100 = $ _____

   $5 \times 1,000 = $ _____

9. $8 \times 60 = $ _____

   $8 \times 600 = $ _____

   $8 \times 6,000 = $ _____

10. $7 \times 90 = $ _____

    $7 \times 900 = $ _____

    $7 \times 9,000 = $ _____

11. Mr. Allen buys 3,000 boxes of stickers for his store. Each box contains 6 packs of stickers. How many packs of stickers does Mr. Allen buy?

_____

Multiply by 1-Digit Numbers
Skill 12

Objective
To multiply 1-digit numbers by 2-, 3-, or 4-digit numbers

COMMON ERROR

- When using place value and regrouping, students may multiply the digits of a multi-digit factor from left to right instead of from least value to greatest value.

- To correct this, remind students that in order to regroup across place values, they should first multiply the digits with the least value. Have students write the multiplication for the ones, tens, hundreds, and thousands in each problem to emphasize the value of each digit.

Learn the Math page IN47 Read the problem aloud with students. Point out that when using place value and regrouping to multiply, you start with the ones. Guide students through Steps 1–3. Ask: **What is the product of 5 and 146?** 730 **How does the product compare to your estimate?** Possible answer: the product 730 is close to the estimate 750.

REASONING Discuss the problem with the class. Then have students use the same reasoning to find the product of 5 and 147. Ask: **Will the product of 5 and 147 be greater or less than 5 × 145? How do you know?** Possible answer: the product will be greater because there are two more groups of 5.

Do the Math page IN48 Discuss Exercise 1 with students. Guide them through regrouping the ones and adding the regrouped tens. Discuss that the steps in multiplying with a 4-digit number are nearly the same as multiplying with a 3-digit number. There is one more step: to multiply the thousands.

Assign Exercises 2–9 and monitor students' work. Encourage them to find estimates first and to check the product by comparing it to the estimate.

Discuss Problem 10 with students. Invite volunteers to answer the following questions. Ask: **What factors will you multiply?** 7 and 1,675 **What estimate can you make?** Possible answer: 7 × 2,000 = 14,000 **Which place-value positions will you need to regroup when multiplying?** ones, tens, and hundreds **How many sheets of paper does Mrs. Barker buy altogether?** 11,725 sheets of paper

Students who make more than 2 errors in Exercises 1–10 may benefit from the **Alternative Teaching Strategy**.

Alternative Teaching Strategy
Manipulatives: base-ten blocks

Give each pair of students a set of hundreds, tens, and ones base-ten blocks. Write 4 × 52 on the board. Discuss the place value of each digit in the two-digit factor. Have each pair of students model 52 four times using base-ten blocks. Tell students to add the tens and the ones in 52 + 52 + 52 + 52. 20 tens 8 ones To solve, have students regroup to rename the sum. Students should regroup 20 tens as 2 hundreds. Help students conclude that the repeated addition shows 4 groups of 52, so 4 × 52 = 208. Repeat with similar problems.

Name _____

Learn the Math

Mr. Sampson drives 146 miles a week. If he drives the same number of miles every week, how many miles does he drive in 5 weeks?

You can use place value and regrouping to multiply.

Multiply 5×146.   Estimate $5 \times 150 = $ __750__

Step 1 Multiply the ones. 5×6 ones = __30__ ones Regroup 30 ones as 3 tens 0 ones.	$\begin{array}{r} 3 \\ 146 \\ \times\ 5 \\ \hline 0 \end{array}$ Regroup 30 ones as 3 tens 0 ones.
Step 2 Multiply the tens. 5×4 tens = __20__ tens Add the regrouped tens. 20 tens + 3 tens = __23__ tens Regroup 23 tens as 2 hundreds 3 tens.	$\begin{array}{r} 2\ 3 \\ 146 \\ \times\ 5 \\ \hline 30 \end{array}$ Regroup 23 tens as 2 hundreds 3 tens.
Step 3 Multiply the hundreds. 5×1 hundred = __5__ hundreds Add the regrouped hundreds. 5 hundreds + 2 hundreds = __7__ hundreds	$\begin{array}{r} 2\ 3 \\ 146 \\ \times\ 5 \\ \hline 730 \end{array}$

So, Mr. Sampson drives __730__ miles in 5 weeks.

REASONING Is 5×145 greater than or less than 730? Explain your answer.

**Less than 730; possible answer: since 145 is less than
146, I know that the product of 5 × 145 has one less
group of 5 than the product of 5 × 146.**

---

1. Last week Mr. Ramey drove his delivery truck 2,018 miles. If he drives this many miles every week, how many miles does he drive in 4 weeks?

   Multiply. $4 \times 2,018$ Estimate. $4 \times 2,000 = $ __8,000__

   - Multiply the ones. Regroup. $\begin{array}{r} 3 \\ 2{,}018 \\ \times\ \ 4 \\ \hline 2 \end{array}$

   - Multiply the tens. Add the regrouped tens. $\begin{array}{r} 3 \\ 2{,}018 \\ \times\ \ 4 \\ \hline 7\,2 \end{array}$

   - Multiply the hundreds. $\begin{array}{r} 3 \\ 2{,}018 \\ \times\ \ 4 \\ \hline 0\,72 \end{array}$

   - Multiply the thousands. $\begin{array}{r} 3 \\ 2{,}018 \\ \times\ \ 4 \\ \hline 8\,072 \end{array}$

   So, Mr. Ramey drives __8,072__ miles in 4 weeks.

Remember

When using place value and regrouping, multiply the digits in order. Start with the digit that has the least value, the digit in the ones place.

Find the product.

2. $\begin{array}{r} 35 \\ \times\ 8 \\ \hline 280 \end{array}$	3. $\begin{array}{r} 49 \\ \times\ 9 \\ \hline 441 \end{array}$	4. $\begin{array}{r} 219 \\ \times\ 3 \\ \hline 657 \end{array}$	5. $\begin{array}{r} \$746 \\ \times\ 8 \\ \hline \$5{,}968 \end{array}$
6. $\begin{array}{r} 199 \\ \times\ 5 \\ \hline 995 \end{array}$	7. $\begin{array}{r} 6{,}291 \\ \times\ 4 \\ \hline 25{,}164 \end{array}$	8. $\begin{array}{r} 8{,}057 \\ \times\ 7 \\ \hline 56{,}399 \end{array}$	9. $\begin{array}{r} 1{,}747 \\ \times\ 6 \\ \hline 10{,}482 \end{array}$

10. Mrs. Barker buys 7 boxes of paper. Each box of paper has 1,675 sheets of paper. How many sheets of paper does Mrs. Barker buy altogether?

   11,725 sheets of paper

Name _____

Learn the Math

Mr. Sampson drives 146 miles a week. If he drives the same number of miles every week, how many miles does he drive in 5 weeks?

You can use place value and regrouping to multiply.

Multiply 5×146.   Estimate $5 \times 150 =$ _____.

Step 1 Multiply the ones. 5×6 ones = _____ ones Regroup 30 ones as 3 tens 0 ones.	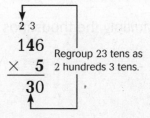 146 × 5 0 Regroup 30 ones as 3 tens 0 ones.
Step 2 Multiply the tens. 5×4 tens = _____ tens Add the regrouped tens. 20 tens + 3 tens = _____ tens Regroup 23 tens as 2 hundreds 3 tens.	2 3 146 × 5 30 Regroup 23 tens as 2 hundreds 3 tens.
Step 3 Multiply the hundreds. 5×1 hundred = _____ hundreds Add the regrouped hundreds. 5 hundreds + 2 hundreds = _____ hundreds	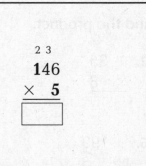 2 3 146 × 5

So, Mr. Sampson drives _____ miles in 5 weeks.

REASONING Is 5×145 greater than or less than 730? Explain your answer.

_____

_____

_____

1. Last week Mr. Ramey drove his delivery truck 2,018 miles. If he drives this many miles every week, how many miles does he drive in 4 weeks?

   Multiply. 4 × 2,018   Estimate. 4 × 2,000 = _____

Remember
When using place value and regrouping, multiply the digits in order. Start with the digit that has the least value, the digit in the ones place.

   - Multiply the ones.
     Regroup.

     $\square$

     2,01**8**
     ×   **4**
     _____
     $\square$

   - Multiply the tens.
     Add the regrouped tens.

     ³
     2,0**1**8
     ×   **4**
     _____
     $\square$2

   - Multiply the hundreds.

     ³
     2,**0**18
     ×   **4**
     _____
     $\square$72

   - Multiply the thousands.

     ³
     2,018
     ×   **4**
     _____
     $\square$,072

   So, Mr. Ramey drives _____ miles in 4 weeks.

Find the product.

2. 35	3. 49	4. 219	5. $746
× 8	× 9	× 3	× 8

6. 199	7. 6,291	8. 8,057	9. 1,747
× 5	× 4	× 7	× 6

10. Mrs. Barker buys 7 boxes of paper. Each box of paper has 1,675 sheets of paper. How many sheets of paper does Mrs. Barker buy altogether?

_____

Subtract Through 4-Digit Numbers
Skill 13

Objective
To subtract through 4-digit numbers

COMMON ERROR

- Students may forget to rename numbers properly when regrouping in subtraction.

- To correct this, remind students to regroup from the next greater place-value position to the lesser place-value position.

Learn the Math page IN51 Read the problem with students. Ask: **How do you know which operation to use to solve this problem?** The problem asks how many more, so I know to subtract. Guide students through each step. Ask: **Why is it necessary to regroup in Step 1?** Possible answer: there are not enough ones to subtract because 9 ones > 2 ones. **Why is it necessary to regroup in Step 3?** Possible answer: there are not enough hundreds to subtract because 8 hundreds > 3 hundreds.

REASONING Help students understand the 10-to-1 relationship between a place-value position and the next greater position to aid in regrouping. Emphasize that regrouping does not change the value of the number. For example, 5,000 shown as 4,990 and 10 ones is the same value as 5,000.

Do the Math page IN52 Read and discuss Exercise 1 with students. Ask: **What do you need to find?** how many more cans Kim collects than Andrew Guide students through each bulleted

step. In the second step, remind students to compare 8 tens to 2 tens, not 3 tens. In the third step, discuss that there are no hundreds because 1 hundred was regrouped as 10 tens + 2 tens to subtract the tens.

Assign Exercises 2–9 and monitor students' work.

Discuss Problem 10 with students. Ask: **How can you find the answer?** Subtract 4,625 − 1,847. Instruct students to write this as a vertical subtraction problem. Ask: **What place-value positions do you need to regroup?** tens, hundreds, and thousands **How do you know?** Possible answer: the digits of the subtrahend (bottom number) are greater than the digits of the minuend (top number) in the ones, tens, and hundreds places. So, I need to regroup from the next greater place-value position. **What is the difference?** 2,778

Students who make more than 2 errors in Exercises 1–10 may benefit from the **Alternative Teaching Strategy**.

Alternative Teaching Strategy
Combine place-value positions to subtract. Write the problem 4,936 − 841 as a vertical subtraction problem. Have students copy the problem and guide them through the following steps to solve. First, subtract the ones. $6 - 1 = 5$ Record the 5 in the ones place. Since $4 > 3$, combine the tens and hundreds places to subtract. $93 - 84 = 9$ Record the 9 in the tens place and a zero in the hundreds place. Subtract the thousands. $4 - 0 = 4$ Record the 4 in the thousands place. Ask: **What is the difference between 4,936 and 841?** 4,095 Repeat with similar problems. Vary the place-value positions that need to be regrouped in additional examples.

Name _____

Learn the Math

Last year, 859 students volunteered to help with the school fundraiser. This year, 2,372 students volunteered. How many more students volunteered this year?

You can use place value to subtract.

Subtract 2,372 − 859.

Step 1 Subtract the ones. Since 9 > 2, you need to regroup. 7 tens 2 ones = 6 tens 12 ones __12__ ones − __9__ ones = __3__ ones	6 12 2,3 7 2 − 8 5 9 ⎿3⏌
Step 2 Subtract the tens. __6__ tens − __5__ tens = __1__ ten	6 12 2,3 7 2 − 8 5 9 ⎿1⏌3
Step 3 Regroup to subtract the hundreds. 2 thousands 3 hundreds = 1 thousand 13 hundreds __13__ hundreds − __8__ hundreds = __5__ hundreds	1 13 6 12 2,3 7 2 − 8 5 9 ⎿5⏌1 3
Step 4 Subtract the thousands. __1__ thousand − __0__ thousands = __1__ thousand	1 13 6 12 2,3 7 2 − 8 5 9 ⎿1⏌,5 1 3

So, __1,513__ more students volunteered this year.

REASONING Pete needs to find the difference between 1,234 and 909. Explain which places need to be regrouped.

Possible answer: since 9 ones > 4 ones, regroup 3 tens 4 ones as 2 tens 14 ones. Since 9 hundreds > 2 hundreds, regroup 1 thousand 2 hundreds as 0 thousands 12 hundreds.

Do the Math

1. Kim collects 132 aluminum cans. Andrew collects 84 aluminum cans. How many more cans does Kim collect?

Subtract. 132 − 84

- Subtract the ones.

  Since 4 > 2, you need to regroup.

  3 tens 2 ones = 2 tens, __12__ ones

  __12__ ones − __4__ ones = __8__ ones

  2 12
1 3 2
− 8 4
8

- Subtract the tens.

  Since 8 tens > 2 tens, you need to regroup.

  1 hundred 2 tens = 0 hundreds __12__ tens

  __12__ tens − __8__ tens = __4__ tens

  12
0 2 12
1 3 2
− 8 4
⎿4⏌8

- There are no hundreds left to subtract.

So, Kim collects __48__ more cans.

Find the difference.

2. 516 − 29 **487**	3. 626 − 8 **618**	4. 1,627 − 559 **1,068**	5. 8,415 − 531 **7,884**
6. 2,473 − 196 **2,277**	7. 5,413 − 834 **4,579**	8. 644 − 36 **608**	9. 195 − 9 **186**

10. In October, Ms. Tyndall's class read a total of 1,847 pages. In November, the class read a total of 4,625 pages. How many more pages did Ms. Tyndall's class read in November than in October?

2,778 pages

Name _____

Learn the Math

Last year, 859 students volunteered to help with the school fundraiser. This year, 2,372 students volunteered. How many more students volunteered this year?

You can use place value to subtract.

Subtract 2,372 − 859.

Step 1 Subtract the ones. Since 9 > 2, you need to regroup. 7 tens 2 ones = 6 tens 12 ones _____ ones − _____ ones = _____ ones	$\begin{array}{r} {\scriptstyle 6\ 12} \\ 2,3\,7\,2 \\ -\ \ 8\,5\,9 \\ \hline \square \end{array}$
Step 2 Subtract the tens. _____ tens − _____ tens = _____ ten	$\begin{array}{r} {\scriptstyle 6\ 12} \\ 2,3\,7\,2 \\ -\ \ 8\,5\,9 \\ \hline \square 3 \end{array}$
Step 3 Regroup to subtract the hundreds. 2 thousands 3 hundreds = 1 thousand 13 hundreds _____ hundreds − _____ hundreds = _____ hundreds	$\begin{array}{r} {\scriptstyle 1\ 13\ 6\ 12} \\ 2,3\,7\,2 \\ -\ \ 8\,5\,9 \\ \hline \square 1\,3 \end{array}$
Step 4 Subtract the thousands. _____ thousand − _____ thousands = _____ thousand	$\begin{array}{r} {\scriptstyle 1\ 13\ 6\ 12} \\ 2,3\,7\,2 \\ -\ \ 8\,5\,9 \\ \hline \square,5\,1\,3 \end{array}$

So, _____ more students volunteered this year.

REASONING Pete needs to find the difference between 1,234 and 909. Explain which places need to be regrouped.

_____

_____

_____

1. Kim collects 132 aluminum cans. Andrew collects 84 aluminum cans. How many more cans does Kim collect?

Subtract. $132 - 84$

- Subtract the ones.

  Since $4 > 2$, you need to regroup.

  3 tens 2 ones = 2 tens, _____ ones

  _____ ones − _____ ones = _____ ones

$$\begin{array}{r} \square\square \\ 1\,3\!\!\!/\,2\!\!\!/ \\ -\ 8\,4 \\ \hline \square \end{array}$$

- Subtract the tens.

  Since 8 tens > 2 tens, you need to regroup.

  1 hundred 2 tens = 0 hundreds _____ tens

  _____ tens − _____ tens = _____ tens

$$\begin{array}{r} \square \\ \square\ \ {}^{2}\!\!\!/\,{}^{12} \\ 1\!\!\!/\,3\!\!\!/\,2\!\!\!/ \\ -\ 8\,4 \\ \hline \square\,8 \end{array}$$

- There are no hundreds left to subtract.

So, Kim collects _____ more cans.

Find the difference.

2.
$$\begin{array}{r} 516 \\ -\ 29 \\ \hline \end{array}$$

3.
$$\begin{array}{r} 626 \\ -\ 8 \\ \hline \end{array}$$

4.
$$\begin{array}{r} 1,627 \\ -\ 559 \\ \hline \end{array}$$

5.
$$\begin{array}{r} 8,415 \\ -\ 531 \\ \hline \end{array}$$

6.
$$\begin{array}{r} 2,473 \\ -\ 196 \\ \hline \end{array}$$

7.
$$\begin{array}{r} 5,413 \\ -\ 834 \\ \hline \end{array}$$

8.
$$\begin{array}{r} 644 \\ -\ 36 \\ \hline \end{array}$$

9.
$$\begin{array}{r} 195 \\ -\ 9 \\ \hline \end{array}$$

10. In October, Ms. Tyndall's class read a total of 1,847 pages. In November, the class read a total of 4,625 pages. How many more pages did Ms. Tyndall's class read in November than in October?

_____

Objective
To subtract 3- and 4-digit numbers across zeros

COMMON ERROR

- Students may not regroup, but may simply subtract zero from the bottom number.
- To correct this, have students compare the top and bottom digit in each place-value position before they subtract.

Learn the Math page IN55 Read the problem aloud to students. In Step 1, ask: **Do you have enough ones to subtract?** no **Can you regroup tens as ones? Explain.** No, there are no tens. **Can you regroup hundreds as tens?** No, there are no hundreds. Discuss that you first regroup from the thousands place. Guide students through regrouping in each place-value position.

REASONING Elicit that since you cannot regroup the tens or hundreds, then you must start regrouping from the thousands place. The three place-value positions that you regroup are the thousands place, the hundreds place, and the tens place.

Do the Math page IN56 Read Exercise 1 aloud to students. Ask: **What place-value positions do you regroup? Explain.** Thousands, hundreds, and tens; possible answer: since there are not enough ones to subtract, I need to regroup. Since there are no tens or hundreds, I need to start with the thousands and then regroup the hundreds and then the tens.

Assign Exercises 2–13 and monitor students' work.

Discuss Problem 14 with the students. Instruct them to write the problem as a vertical subtraction problem. Ask: **Are there enough ones to subtract?** no **How do you know?** 8 ones > 6 ones **Explain how to regroup to subtract.** First I regroup 1 hundred 0 tens as 0 hundreds 10 tens, and then I regroup 10 tens 6 ones as 9 tens 16 ones. **What is the difference?** 48 Repeat with similar questions for Problem 15.

Students who make more than 4 errors in Exercises 1–15 may benefit from the **Alternative Teaching Strategy**.

Alternative Teaching Strategy
Manipulatives: base-ten blocks

Have students work together in pairs using base-ten blocks. Ask one student to model numbers using the blocks while the other records each step with paper and pencil. Write 506 − 27 on the board. Have students model 506 using base-ten blocks. Guide them to recognize that they cannot subtract the ones until they regroup the hundreds. Instruct them to regroup 5 hundreds 0 tens as 4 hundreds 10 tens and then to regroup 10 tens 6 ones as 9 tens 16 ones. Have them remove 2 tens and 7 ones and record the difference of 479. Repeat with similar problems.

Learn the Math

Jonas needs 2,000 points to make it to the next level of his video game. He has 789 points. How many more points does he need?

You can use place value to subtract across zeros.

Subtract. 2,000 − 789

Step 1	
Subtract the ones. Since 9 > 0, regroup tens. There are no tens or hundreds, so regroup thousands. 2 thousands 0 hundreds = __1__ thousand __10__ hundreds	1 10 2,0̸00 − 789
Step 2	
Regroup hundreds. 10 hundreds 0 tens = __9__ hundreds __10__ tens	9 1 1̸0̸ 10 2,0̸0̸0 − 789
Step 3	
Regroup tens. 10 tens 0 ones = __9__ tens __10__ ones	9 9 1 1̸0̸ 1̸0̸10 2,0̸0̸0 − 789
Step 4	
Subtract the ones. Subtract the tens. Subtract the hundreds, and subtract the thousands.	9 9 1 1̸0̸ 1̸0̸10 2,0̸0̸0̸ − 789 **1,211**

So, Jonas needs __1,211__ points to make it to the next level of his video game.

REASONING Explain why you need to regroup three times to find 2,000 − 789.

Possible answer: you cannot subtract from 0 ones and there are no tens or hundreds you can use to regroup. So, you start by regrouping thousands.

Do the Math

Skill ⓵

Remember
Start regrouping from the place-value position of the least value that does not have a zero in it.

1. Abby asks for 1,002 items to be added to the school supply store. She is given 874 items. What is the difference between what Abby asks for and what she is given?

• Write the subtraction problem. __1,002 − 874__
• Do you need to regroup to subtract? __yes__
• How many times will you regroup? __3__ times

```
      9 9
  0 1̸0 1̸0 12
  1,0̸0̸2̸
  −  874
    128
```

So, Abby is given __128__ fewer items.

Find the difference.

2. 106 − 37 **69**	3. 600 − 8 **592**	4. 904 − 66 **838**	5. 205 − 7 **198**
6. 400 − 98 **302**	7. 505 − 119 **386**	8. 9,003 − 412 **8,591**	9. 5,100 − 588 **4,512**
10. 2,094 − 405 **1,689**	11. 5,000 − 913 **4,087**	12. 3,070 − 832 **2,238**	13. 5,004 − 2,987 **2,017**

14. There are 106 dogs and cats at the animal fair. There are 58 dogs. How many cats are there?

__48 cats__

15. There were 1,000 student tickets to the animal fair sold and 784 adult tickets sold. How many more student tickets were sold?

__216 tickets__

Name _____

Learn the Math

Jonas needs 2,000 points to make it to the next level of his video game. He has 789 points. How many more points does he need?

You can use place value to subtract across zeros.

Subtract. 2,000 − 789

Step 1 Subtract the ones. Since 9 > 0, regroup tens. There are no tens or hundreds, so regroup thousands. 2 thousands 0 hundreds = _____ thousand _____ hundreds	1 10 2̶,Ø 0 0 − 7 8 9
Step 2 Regroup hundreds. 10 hundreds 0 tens = _____ hundreds _____ tens	9 1 1̶0̶ 10 2̶,Ø 0 0 − 7 8 9
Step 3 Regroup tens. 10 tens 0 ones = _____ tens _____ ones	9 9 1 1̶0̶ 1̶0̶ 10 2̶,Ø 0 0 − 7 8 9
Step 4 Subtract the ones. Subtract the tens. Subtract the hundreds, and subtract the thousands.	9 9 1 1̶0̶ 1̶0̶ 10 2̶,Ø Ø Ø − 7 8 9 ☐

So, Jonas needs _____ points to make it to the next level of his video game.

REASONING Explain why you need to regroup three times to find 2,000 − 789.

_____

_____

_____

1. Abby asks for 1,002 items to be added to the school supply store. She is given 874 items. What is the difference between what Abby asks for and what she is given?

   - Write the subtraction problem. _____

   - Do you need to regroup to subtract? _____

   - How many times will you regroup? _____ times

```
      0 10 10
   1, 0 0 2
 -    8 7 4
   ┌────┐
   └────┘
```

So, Abby is given _____ fewer items.

Find the difference.

2. 106 − 37	3. 600 − 8	4. 904 − 66	5. 205 − 7
6. 400 − 98	7. 505 − 119	8. 9,003 − 412	9. 5,100 − 588
10. 2,094 − 405	11. 5,000 − 913	12. 3,070 − 832	13. 5,004 − 2,987

14. There are 106 dogs and cats at the animal fair. There are 58 dogs. How many cats are there?

_____

15. There were 1,000 student tickets to the animal fair sold and 784 adult tickets sold. How many more student tickets were sold?

_____

Multiples
Skill 15

Objective
To find multiples using a number line or a multiplication table

Vocabulary
multiple A number that is the product of two counting numbers

Materials
number lines, multiplication table (see *Teacher Resources*)

COMMON ERROR

- Students may skip the first multiple when writing a list of multiples for a given number.

- To correct this, have students use a number line to skip count. Remind them to begin at 0 and list all of the numbers on which they stop while skip counting. The first number, or the first multiple, will always be the product of 1 and the number.

Learn the Math page IN59 For Example 1, have students trace the first jump of 4 on the number line, and then draw four more jumps of 4. As they draw each jump, count aloud with students.

Discuss the definition of a multiple and that each number they stopped on while skip counting is a multiple of 4.

For Example 2, have students shade the row or the column for the factor 9 in the multiplication table. Ask: **What does the shaded row or column show?** the multiples of 9 **What are the first twelve multiples of 9?** 9, 18, 27, 36, 45, 54, 63, 72, 81, 90, 99, and 108

REASONING Discuss that skip counting by threes on a number line is a way to show multiplication. Each jump of 3 shows the product of 3 and a counting number.

Do the Math page IN60 Read the problem aloud with students. Ask: **By what number will you skip count?** 6 Have students skip count by sixes on the number line. Ask: **How did you know to stop on 24?** Possible answer: the next multiple, 30, is greater than the number of players on the team. Have students list the first four multiples of 6. Assist them as they identify the ordinal number for each student assigned a ball-handling drill.

Assign Exercises 2–9 and monitor students' work. Instruct them to draw jumps on the number lines in Exercises 2 and 3.

Discuss Problems 10 and 11 with students. Ask: **You need to find multiples of what number to solve Problem 10?** 6 **How many multiples of 6 do you need to find?** the first four multiples Ask similar questions about Problem 11.

Students who make more than 3 errors in Exercises 1–11 may benefit from the **Alternative Teaching Strategy**.

Alternative Teaching Strategy
Manipulatives: counters

Have students work in pairs with sets of counters. Ask them to find the first five multiples of 7 using counters. Direct them to arrange the counters into five groups of 7 counters each. Have them record the multiples of 7 after they finish counting each group. Then have them identify the first five multiples of 7 by listing the numbers that they have recorded. Repeat to find multiples of other numbers.

Multiples
Skill **15**

Learn the Math

Jonathan has 5 pages with 4 stickers on each page in his sticker book. How many stickers does he have in all?

Example 1 Use a number line.

Draw 5 jumps for the pages of stickers.

Jump 4 spaces at a time for the number of stickers on each page.

Vocabulary

multiple

0   4   8   12   16   20

Skip count by fours 5 times. 4, __8__ __12__ __16__ __20__

The numbers you counted are multiples of 4. A **multiple** of a number is a product of the number and a counting number.

So, Jonathan has __20__ stickers in all.

Example 2 Use a multiplication table.

Write the first twelve multiples of 9.

To find multiples of 9, look at the row or the column for the factor 9.

Shade the row or the column for the factor 9.

The first twelve multiples of 9 are __9__,
__18__ __27__ __36__ __45__ __54__
__63__ __72__ __81__ __90__ __99__
and __108__.

×	1	2	3	4	5	6	7	8	9	10	11	12
1	1	2	3	4	5	6	7	8	9	10	11	12
2	2	4	6	8	10	12	14	16	18	20	22	24
3	3	6	9	12	15	18	21	24	27	30	33	36
4	4	8	12	16	20	24	28	32	36	40	44	48
5	5	10	15	20	25	30	35	40	45	50	55	60
6	6	12	18	24	30	36	42	48	54	60	66	72
7	7	14	21	28	35	42	49	56	63	70	77	84
8	8	16	24	32	40	48	56	64	72	80	88	96
9	9	18	27	36	45	54	63	72	81	90	99	108
10	10	20	30	40	50	60	70	80	90	100	110	120
11	11	22	33	44	55	66	77	88	99	110	121	132
12	12	24	36	48	60	72	84	96	108	120	132	144

REASONING How is skip counting by threes 6 times the same as writing the first six multiples of 3?

Possible answer: both represent the
products of 3 × 1, 3 × 2, 3 × 3, 3 × 4,
3 × 5, and 3 × 6.

Response to Intervention • Tier 2 **IN59**

Do the Math

Skill **15**

1. As players walk onto the gym floor, the coach assigns every sixth player a ball-handling drill. There are 25 players on the team. Which players are assigned a ball-handling drill?

- Skip count by __6__ to find each player assigned a ball-handling drill.

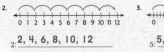

0 1 2 3 4 5 6 7 8 9 10 11 12 13 14 15 16 17 18 19 20 21 22 23 24 25

- What are the first four multiples of 6? __6__, __12__, __18__, and __24__

So, the 6th, __12__th, __18__th, and __24__th players are assigned a ball-handling drill.

Remember

A multiple of a number is a product of that number and a counting number.

Write the first six multiples of each number.

2.
0 1 2 3 4 5 6 7 8 9 10 11 12

__2, 4, 6, 8, 10, 12__

3.
0 5 10 15 20 25 30

__5, 10, 15, 20, 25, 30__

4. 3: __3, 6, 9, 12, 15, 18__

5. 8: __8, 16, 24, 32, 40, 48__

6. 7: __7, 14, 21, 28, 35, 42__

7. 10: __10, 20, 30, 40, 50, 60__

8. 4: __4, 8, 12, 16, 20, 24__

9. 12: __12, 24, 36, 48, 60, 72__

10. The library sells erasers in packs of 6. Write the number of erasers you will have if you buy 1 pack, 2 packs, 3 packs, and 4 packs.

__6 erasers, 12 erasers, 18 erasers, 24 erasers__

11. The book store sells pencils in packs of 4. How many pencils will you have if you buy 8 packs? Write the first eight multiples of 4 to solve.

__32 pencils; 4, 8, 12, 16, 20, 24, 28, 32__

IN60 Response to Intervention • Tier 2

Name _____

Learn the Math

Jonathan has 5 pages with 4 stickers on each page in his sticker book. How many stickers does he have in all?

Example 1 Use a number line.

Draw 5 jumps for the pages of stickers.

Jump 4 spaces at a time for the number of stickers on each page.

Skip count by fours 5 times. 4, _____, _____, _____, _____

The numbers you counted are multiples of 4. A **multiple** of a number is a product of the number and a counting number.

So, Jonathan has _____ stickers in all.

Example 2 Use a multiplication table.

Write the first twelve multiples of 9.

To find multiples of 9, look at the row or the column for the factor 9.

Shade the row or the column for the factor 9.

The first twelve multiples of 9 are _____,

_____, _____, _____, _____, _____,

_____, _____, _____, _____, _____,

and _____.

×	1	2	3	4	5	6	7	8	9	10	11	12
1	1	2	3	4	5	6	7	8	9	10	11	12
2	2	4	6	8	10	12	14	16	18	20	22	24
3	3	6	9	12	15	18	21	24	27	30	33	36
4	4	8	12	16	20	24	28	32	36	40	44	48
5	5	10	15	20	25	30	35	40	45	50	55	60
6	6	12	18	24	30	36	42	48	54	60	66	72
7	7	14	21	28	35	42	49	56	63	70	77	84
8	8	16	24	32	40	48	56	64	72	80	88	96
9	9	18	27	36	45	54	63	72	81	90	99	108
10	10	20	30	40	50	60	70	80	90	100	110	120
11	11	22	33	44	55	66	77	88	99	110	121	132
12	12	24	36	48	60	72	84	96	108	120	132	144

REASONING How is skip counting by threes 6 times the same as writing the first six multiples of 3?

_____

_____

_____

Do the Math

Skill **15**

Remember
A multiple of a number is a product of that number and a counting number.

1. As players walk onto the gym floor, the coach assigns every sixth player a ball-handling drill. There are 25 players on the team. Which players are assigned a ball-handling drill?

   • Skip count by _____ to find each player assigned a ball-handling drill.

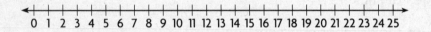

   • What are the first four multiples of 6? _____, _____, _____, and _____.

   So, the 6th, _____th, _____th, and _____th players are assigned a ball-handling drill.

Write the first six multiples of each number.

2.

   2: _____

4. 3: _____

6. 7: _____

8. 4: _____

3.

   5: _____

5. 8: _____

7. 10: _____

9. 12: _____

10. The library sells erasers in packs of 6. Write the number of erasers you will have if you buy 1 pack, 2 packs, 3 packs, and 4 packs.

   _____

11. The book store sells pencils in packs of 4. How many pencils will you have if you buy 8 packs? Write the first eight multiples of 4 to solve.

   _____

© Houghton Mifflin Harcourt Publishing Company

Objective
To read and interpret data in a pictograph

Vocabulary

pictograph A graph that uses small pictures or symbols to show information

key The part of a map or a graph that explains what the symbols represent

COMMON ERROR

- Students may forget to read the key before they read the pictograph.

- To correct this, have students circle the key and read it aloud.

Learn the Math page IN63 Read the problem with students.

Discuss the pictograph and how the data are organized. Help students identify the parts of the pictograph such as the title, the row labels, and the key.

Emphasize the importance of reading the key to understand what each symbol represents. Ask: **What does each book stand for?** 4 books Ask: **What does a half book stand for?** 2 books

Show students how to read the graph to determine how many books Torrie read.

Say: **You can count the number of books by fours. Then add 2 for a half book.** Ask: **How many books did Torrie read?** 18 books

REASONING Discuss the question with the students. Then ask: **Suppose there were no key in the pictograph about books. Are there any conclusions you can draw without a key?** Possible answer: I could make comparisons, such as who read the most books, but I could not answer questions about actual numbers.

Do the Math page IN64 Read and discuss Exercise 1 with students.

Ask: **What does the key tell you about the pictograph?** Each whole symbol in the pictograph stands for 10 tickets.

Ask: **What does a half ticket stand for?** 5 tickets Model how to skip count by tens and then add 5 to solve the problem.

Assign Exercises 2–6 and monitor students' work.

Discuss Problem 7. Ask: **How many snowflakes would you need for snowboarding if 1 snowflake stood for 10 votes?** 20 snowflakes Ask: **Would it be easy to read the pictograph?** Possible answer: no, it would be too long.

Students who make more than 1 error in Exercises 1–7 may benefit from the **Alternative Teaching Strategy**.

Alternative Teaching Strategy
Materials: 1-inch grid paper (see *Teacher Resources*)

Have groups of students survey classmates on their favorite colors, giving four possible answer choices. Then have each group create a pictograph of their data. Say: **Look at your data and determine a key and a symbol.** Ask each group: **How many votes should each symbol in your pictograph stand for?** Accept reasonable responses. Guide students to make pictographs on grid paper, using the grids as guides. Remind students to include a key. Students can write questions about their pictographs, trade their questions with another group, and answer the other group's questions.

Name _____

Learn the Math

Mrs. Martin asks the students in her class about the number of books they read during summer vacation. She makes a pictograph to show the number of books some students read. How many books did Torrie read during summer vacation?

A **pictograph** uses pictures or symbols to show information. Look at the **key** to see what each symbol represents.

Books Read During Summer Vacation

Kay	📖 📖 📖 📖
Derek	📖 📖
Sydney	📖 📖 📖 📖 📖
Torrie	📖 📖 📖 📖 📖
Nick	📖 📖 📖

Key: Each 📖 = 4 books.

- The title tells us that the pictograph is about the number of books read during summer vacation.

- Each row has a label that tells the name of the student.

- The key tells that each symbol stands for 4 books. A 📖 stands for 2 since 📖 stands for 4.

To find the number of books that Torrie read during summer vacation, count the number of 📖 by fours. Remember to also count the 📖.

$4 + \underline{4} + \underline{4} + \underline{4} + 2 = \underline{18}$

So, Torrie read __18__ books during summer vacation.

REASONING How does the key help you read the pictograph?

Possible answer: the key tells you the quantity
each symbol in the graph represents.

---

1. The drama club sells tickets to the school play. The pictograph shows the number of tickets sold. How many tickets did Alice sell?

Number of Tickets Sold

Jocelyn	🎫 🎫 🎫
Alice	🎫 🎫 🎫 🎟
Marty	🎫 🎫 🎫 🎫 🎟
Kurt	🎫 🎫

Key: Each 🎫 = 10 tickets.

- Each 🎫 equals how many tickets sold? __10__
- Each 🎟 equals how many tickets sold? __5__
So, Alice sold __35__ tickets.

Use the Favorite Winter Activity pictograph for 2–7.

2. Which winter activity received the most votes? __ice skating__

3. How many more people voted for skiing than sleigh riding? __25__

4. How many people voted for skiing and snowboarding combined? __350__

5. How many people voted in all? __800__

6. How many snowflakes would you show in the pictograph if hockey received 175 votes? $3\frac{1}{2}$

7. Would the key ❄ = 10 be a good choice for the pictograph? Explain.

Possible answer: no; the graph would be too large
if each snowflake stood for 10 votes.

Favorite Winter Activity

Ice Skating	❄ ❄ ❄ ❄ ❄
Hockey	❄ ❄
Skiing	❄ ❄ ❄
Sleigh Riding	❄ ❄ ❄
Snowboarding	❄ ❄ ❄ ❄

Key: Each ❄ = 50 votes.

Name _____

Learn the Math

Mrs. Martin asks the students in her class about the number of books they read during summer vacation. She makes a pictograph to show the number of books some students read. How many books did Torrie read during summer vacation?

A **pictograph** uses pictures or symbols to show information. Look at the **key** to see what each symbol represents.

Vocabulary

pictograph
key

Books Read During Summer Vacation	
Kay	📖 📖 📖 📖
Derek	📖 📖 📖
Sydney	📖 📖 📖 📖 📖
Torrie	📖 📖 📖 📖 📖
Nick	📖 📖 📖

Key: Each 📖 **= 4 books.**

- The title tells us that the pictograph is about the number of books read during summer vacation.

- Each row has a label that tells the name of the student.

- The key tells that each symbol stands for 4 books. A 📖 stands for 2 since 📖 stands for 4.

To find the number of books that Torrie read during summer vacation, count the number of 📖 by fours. Remember to also count the 📖 .

$4 + \underline{\quad} + \underline{\quad} + \underline{\quad} + 2 = \underline{\quad}$

So, Torrie read _____ books during summer vacation.

REASONING How does the key help you read the pictograph?

_____

_____

1. The drama club sells tickets to the school play. The pictograph shows the number of tickets sold. How many tickets did Alice sell?

Number of Tickets Sold

Jocelyn	🎭 🎭 🎭
Alice	🎭 🎭 🎭 🎭
Marty	🎭 🎭 🎭 🎭 🎭
Kurt	🎭 🎭

Key: Each 🎭 = 10 tickets.

• Each 🎭 equals how many tickets sold? _____

• Each 🎭 equals how many tickets sold? _____

So, Alice sold _____ tickets.

Use the Favorite Winter Activity pictograph for 2–7.

2. Which winter activity received the most votes? _____

3. How many more people voted for skiing than sleigh riding? _____

4. How many people voted for skiing and snowboarding combined? _____

5. How many people voted in all? _____

6. How many snowflakes would you show in the pictograph if hockey received 175 votes? _____

7. Would the key ❄ = 10 be a good choice for the pictograph? Explain.

Favorite Winter Activity

Ice Skating	❄ ❄ ❄ ❄ ❄
Hockey	❄ ❄
Skiing	❄ ❄ ❄
Sleigh Riding	❄ ❄ ❄
Snowboarding	❄ ❄ ❄ ❄

Key: Each ❄ = 50 votes.

_____

_____

Parts of a Graph
Skill 17

Objective
To know the parts of a bar graph

Vocabulary
horizontal bar graph A bar graph in which the bars go from left to right

scale The equally-spaced numbers on a graph that help identify the value of the data represented

vertical bar graph A bar graph in which the bars go from bottom to top

COMMON ERROR

- Students may forget to read the scale and assume that it increases by ones.

- To correct this, have students circle the scale and skip count from the beginning to the end of the scale.

Learn the Math page IN67 Discuss the problem with students. Work with students to identify the parts of the graph, such as title, scale, and labels. Ask: **What is the scale on this bar graph?** 0–12 Ask: **Does the scale increase by ones?** No, it increases by twos. Discuss the lengths of the bars. Ask: **If one bar is shorter than another, does the shorter bar represent fewer or more votes than the other bar?** fewer votes Ask: **What does the longest bar represent?** Possible answer: the food that received the most votes

Point out to students that they need all parts of the graph in order to read the bars on the graph correctly.

REASONING Discuss the question with

students. After students conclude that data labels are necessary to read the graph, ask: **What if the scale were not shown? What conclusions could you draw about the graph?** Possible answer: I could make comparisons, such as which food got the most votes, but I could not answer questions about the number of votes.

Do the Math page IN68 Read and discuss Exercise 1 with students. Guide students through the description of the bar graph. Ask: **How do you know if the graph is a vertical bar graph or a horizontal bar graph?** Possible answer: I can look to see if the bars go from bottom to top or from left to right.

Assign Exercises 2–6 and monitor students' work.

Discuss Exercise 7. Discuss with students how a horizontal bar graph and a vertical bar graph will have the same parts, but they will be arranged differently. Use the two graphs on the page to discuss the locations of the parts on each graph.

Students who make more than 1 error in Exercises 1–7 may benefit from the **Alternative Teaching Strategy**.

Alternative Teaching Strategy
Materials: 1-inch grid paper (see *Teacher Resources*)

Have groups of students survey their classmates on a topic, giving four possible answer choices. Then have groups create a bar graph of the data. Students should include a title, a scale, and labels. Ask: **How did you decide on a scale for your graph?** Accept reasonable responses. Have students identify the parts of their bar graphs. Discuss what conclusions can be drawn from the graphs.

Name _____

Learn the Math

Max surveys the students in his class about their favorite food. He makes a bar graph to show the results. Which food do the most students choose as their favorite?

A **bar graph** uses bars to show data. On a **horizontal bar graph**, the bars go from left to right. On a **vertical bar graph**, the bars go from bottom to top.

Vocabulary
scale
horizontal bar graph
vertical bar graph

- The *title* tells you what the graph is about.
- The *data label* tells what data are shown.
- A **scale** of equally-spaced numbers helps you read the number each bar shows. The scale on this graph goes from 0–12 by twos.
- The *scale label* tells you what the scale represents.

The length of each bar on this graph shows the number of votes each type of food received. The bar for _pizza_ is the longest.

So, most students choose _pizza_ as their favorite food.

REASONING Why do you need data labels to read a graph?
Possible answer: data labels tell what data are shown on the graph. Without data labels, you would not know what each bar represents.

Response to Intervention • Tier 2 **IN67**

Do the Math

Skill 17

1. Coach Parker started the bar graph below to show the number of students enrolled in sports after school. Describe Coach Parker's graph.

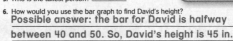

Remember
- Vertical bar graphs and horizontal bar graphs both have all of the same graph parts.
- The scale is the range of equally-spaced numbers that help identify the value of each bar.

- Is this a vertical or a horizontal bar graph? **vertical**
- What is the graph's scale? **0–50 by tens**
- What is the title of the graph? **After-School Sports**
- What is the graph's scale label? **Number of Students**
- What data label would you place at the bottom? **Sport**

Use the bar graph for 2–7.

2. What is the graph's scale label? **Height (in.)**
3. What is the graph's scale? **0–60 by tens**
4. What data label would you place on the left side of the graph? **Family Member**
5. Who is the tallest person? **Maria**
6. How would you use the bar graph to find David's height?
Possible answer: the bar for David is halfway between 40 and 50. So, David's height is 45 in.
7. How would the parts of the bar graph change if you made a vertical bar graph instead of a horizontal bar graph?
Possible answer: the parts would stay the same, but they would be arranged differently.

IN68 Response to Intervention • Tier 2

Name _____

Learn the Math

Max surveys the students in his class about their favorite food. He makes a bar graph to show the results. Which food do the most students choose as their favorite?

A **bar graph** uses bars to show data. On a **horizontal bar graph**, the bars go from left to right. On a **vertical bar graph**, the bars go from bottom to top.

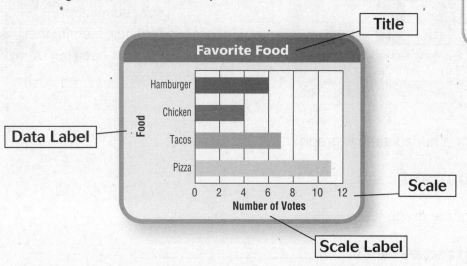

- The *title* tells you what the graph is about.

- The *data label* tells what data are shown.

- A **scale** of equally-spaced numbers helps you read the number each bar shows. The scale on this graph goes from 0–12 by twos.

- The *scale label* tells you what the scale represents.

The length of each bar on this graph shows the number of votes each

type of food received. The bar for _____ is the longest.

So, most students choose _____ as their favorite food.

REASONING Why do you need data labels to read a graph?

_____

_____

_____

1. Coach Parker started the bar graph below to show the number of students enrolled in sports after school. Describe Coach Parker's graph.

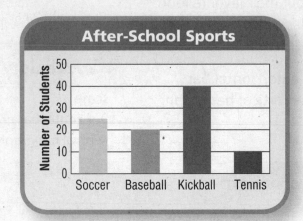

- Is this a vertical or a horizontal bar graph? _____

- What is the graph's scale? _____

- What is the title of the graph? _____

- What is the graph's scale label? _____

- What data label would you place at the bottom? _____

Use the bar graph for 2–7.

2. What is the graph's scale label? _____

3. What is the graph's scale? _____

4. What data label would you place on the left side of the graph? _____

5. Who is the tallest person? _____

6. How would you use the bar graph to find David's height?

_____

_____

7. How would the parts of the bar graph change if you made a vertical bar graph instead of a horizontal bar graph?

_____

_____

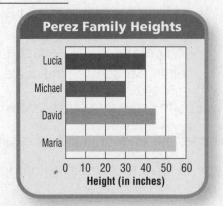

Model Fractions and Mixed Numbers

Skill 18

Objective
To read, write, and model fractions and mixed numbers

Vocabulary
fraction A number that names part of a whole or part of a group

numerator The part of a fraction above the line that tells how many parts are being counted

denominator The part of a fraction below the line that tells how many equal parts there are in the whole or in the group

mixed number A number represented by a whole number and a fraction

COMMON ERROR

- Students may write the number of shaded parts as the numerator, and the number of unshaded parts as the denominator.

- To correct this, have students count the total number of parts and write that number as the denominator before counting the shaded parts to find the numerator.

Learn the Math page IN71 Discuss Example 1 with students. Ask: **How does the model help you write the fraction?** Possible answer: the model shows the total number of equal parts and the number of shaded parts. Discuss Example 2. Ask: **How is this model different from the model in Example 1?** Possible answer: it shows a mixed number.

Explain that a mixed number always has a whole number and a fraction.

REASONING Discuss how to write a fraction greater than one as a mixed number. Ask: **How can you decide if $\frac{3}{2}$ and $1\frac{1}{2}$ are equal?** Possible answer: I can draw a model showing $\frac{3}{2}$ and another model showing $1\frac{1}{2}$ and compare them.

Do the Math page IN72 Read and discuss Exercise 1. Ask: **How do you find the whole number?** Count the number of whole circles that are shaded. **How do you find the denominator of the fraction part of the mixed number?** Count the number of equal parts in one circle.

Assign Exercises 2–9 and monitor students' work.

Discuss Problem 10. Encourage students to draw a model to show the mixed number.

Students who make more than 2 errors in Exercises 1–10 may benefit from the **Alternative Teaching Strategy**.

Alternative Teaching Strategy
Manipulatives and Materials: fraction circles, sandwich bags

Group the fraction circle pieces in bags so that each bag contains a different fraction or mixed number. For example, create sets such as: 2 thirds, 5 sixths, 9 fourths, and so on. Give each pair of students 1 whole circle and two to three bags of fraction circle sets. Have students arrange the pieces in one bag to model a fraction or a mixed number. Remind them to place any pieces that do not make a whole on top of a whole circle. Ask them to write each fraction or mixed number they model. Have pairs repeat with each bag of fraction circle pieces.

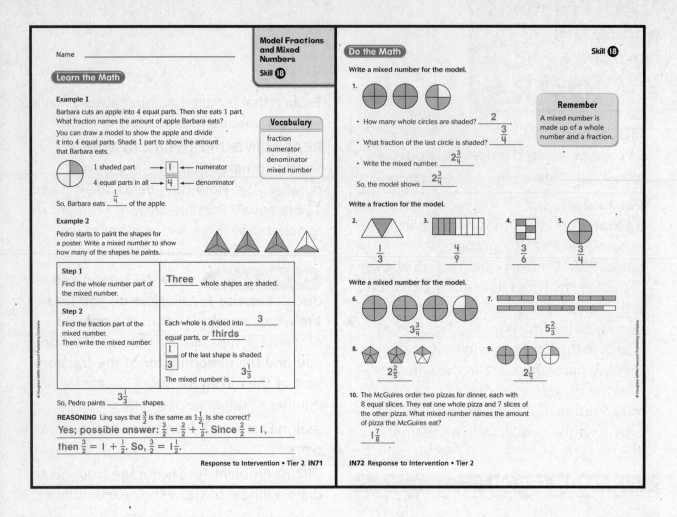

Name _____

Learn the Math

Example 1

Barbara cuts an apple into 4 equal parts. Then she eats 1 part. What fraction names the amount of apple Barbara eats?

You can draw a model to show the apple and divide it into 4 equal parts. Shade 1 part to show the amount that Barbara eats.

1 shaded part → $\boxed{1}$ ← numerator

4 equal parts in all → $\boxed{4}$ ← denominator

So, Barbara eats $\frac{1}{4}$ of the apple.

Vocabulary

fraction
numerator
denominator
mixed number

Example 2

Pedro starts to paint the shapes for a poster. Write a mixed number to show how many of the shapes he paints.

Step 1	
Find the whole number part of the mixed number.	**Three** whole shapes are shaded.
Step 2	
Find the fraction part of the mixed number. Then write the mixed number.	Each whole is divided into ___3___ equal parts, or **thirds** $\frac{1}{3}$ of the last shape is shaded. The mixed number is $3\frac{1}{3}$

So, Pedro paints $3\frac{1}{3}$ shapes.

REASONING Ling says that $\frac{3}{2}$ is the same as $1\frac{1}{2}$. Is she correct?

Yes; possible answer: $\frac{3}{2} = \frac{2}{2} + \frac{1}{2}$. Since $\frac{2}{2} = 1$, then $\frac{3}{2} = 1 + \frac{1}{2}$. So, $\frac{3}{2} = 1\frac{1}{2}$.

Do the Math

Skill 18

Write a mixed number for the model.

1.

- How many whole circles are shaded? ___2___
- What fraction of the last circle is shaded? $\frac{3}{4}$
- Write the mixed number. $2\frac{3}{4}$

So, the model shows $2\frac{3}{4}$.

Remember

A mixed number is made up of a whole number and a fraction.

Write a fraction for the model.

2. $\frac{1}{3}$

3. $\frac{4}{9}$

4. $\frac{3}{6}$

5. $\frac{3}{4}$

Write a mixed number for the model.

6. $3\frac{3}{4}$

7. $5\frac{2}{3}$

8. $2\frac{2}{5}$

9. $2\frac{1}{4}$

10. The McGuires order two pizzas for dinner, each with 8 equal slices. They eat one whole pizza and 7 slices of the other pizza. What mixed number names the amount of pizza the McGuires eat?

$1\frac{7}{8}$

Name _____

Learn the Math

Example 1

Barbara cuts an apple into 4 equal parts. Then she eats 1 part. What fraction names the amount of apple Barbara eats?

You can draw a model to show the apple and divide it into 4 equal parts. Shade 1 part to show the amount that Barbara eats.

Vocabulary

fraction
numerator
denominator
mixed number

1 shaded part ⟶ ☐ ⟵ numerator

4 equal parts in all ⟶ ☐ ⟵ denominator

So, Barbara eats _____ of the apple.

Example 2

Pedro starts to paint the shapes for a poster. Write a mixed number to show how many of the shapes he paints.

Step 1 Find the whole number part of the mixed number.	_____ whole shapes are shaded.
Step 2 Find the fraction part of the mixed number. Then write the mixed number.	Each whole is divided into _____ equal parts, or _____. ☐/☐ of the last shape is shaded. The mixed number is _____.

So, Pedro paints _____ shapes.

REASONING Ling says that $\frac{3}{2}$ is the same as $1\frac{1}{2}$. Is she correct?

_____

_____

Write a mixed number for the model.

1.

- How many whole circles are shaded? _____

- What fraction of the last circle is shaded? _____

- Write the mixed number. _____

So, the model shows _____.

Write a fraction for the model.

2.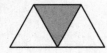

3.

4.

5.

_____   _____   _____   _____

Write a mixed number for the model.

6.

7.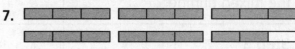

_____

8.

9.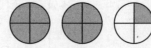

_____   _____

10. The McGuires order two pizzas for dinner, each with
    8 equal slices. They eat one whole pizza and 7 slices of
    the other pizza. What mixed number names the amount
    of pizza the McGuires eat?

_____

Objective
To model and write fractions with denominators of 10

Vocabulary
fraction A number that names part of a whole or part of a group

denominator The part of a fraction below the line, that tells how many equal parts there are in the whole or in the group

numerator The part of a fraction above the line, that tells how many parts are being counted

COMMON ERROR

- Students may incorrectly write a fraction when given its word form.

- To correct this, remind them that the first number named in a fraction is the numerator and the second number named is the denominator.

Learn the Math page IN75 Guide students through the problem. Ask: **How do you know how many parts to shade in the model?** Possible answer: I need to shade 6 parts because I need to show six tenths. Guide students to write the fraction.

REASONING Discuss the question with students. Have students count the unshaded parts on the model to see how many times the coin did not land on tails. Explain to students that the problem could also be solved using mental math: $10 - 6 = 4$. So, $\frac{4}{10}$ represents the number of times the coin landed on heads.

Do the Math page IN76 Read and discuss Exercise 1. Guide students to solve the problem. Ask: **How many parts of the model do you shade to show seven tenths?** 7 parts

Assign Exercises 2–7 and monitor students' work.

For Problem 8, have students draw and shade a model. Discuss that the entire model is shaded, so therefore, $\frac{10}{10}$ is equal to 1 whole.

Discuss Problem 9. Encourage students to draw and shade a model to find half of 10 parts. Ask: **How many parts do you shade?** 5

Students who make more than 2 errors in Exercises 1–9 may benefit from the **Alternative Teaching Strategy**.

Alternative Teaching Strategy
Manipulatives: fraction circles

Give each student a set of fraction circles. Write *seven tenths* on the board. Instruct students to place the whole circle on their desk and then place tenths pieces on top of it to model seven tenths. Ask: **How many tenths pieces do you use?** 7 Ask for a student volunteer to write the fraction $\frac{7}{10}$ on the board. Repeat with other fractions with a denominator of 10.

Name _____

Learn the Math

Althea and Julian flipped a coin 10 times. Julian wrote that six tenths of the flips had an outcome of tails. How can he write six tenths as a fraction?

Step 1

Shade the tenths model to show six tenths.

Step 2

Write a fraction. Write the number of equal parts in all as the denominator and the number of shaded parts as the numerator.

The **numerator** tells how many parts are being counted. The **denominator** tells how many equal parts are in the whole or in the group.

number of shaded parts ⟶ 6 ⟵ numerator
number of equal parts in all ⟶ 10 ⟵ denominator

six tenths = $\frac{6}{10}$

So, the fraction $\frac{6}{10}$ represents the number of times the coin landed on tails.

REASONING Althea says the fraction for the number of times the coin landed on heads is $\frac{4}{10}$. Is she correct? Explain.

Yes; possible answer: the number of times the coin landed on heads is shown by the number of unshaded parts in the model, 4. So, the fraction for the number of times the coin landed on heads is $\frac{4}{10}$.

Response to Intervention • Tier 2 **IN75**

1. Micah won the 100-meter dash by seven tenths of a second. Write seven tenths as a fraction.

 • Shade the model to show seven tenths.

 • How many equal parts are there in all? __10__
 • How many parts are shaded? __7__
 • Write seven tenths as a fraction. __$\frac{7}{10}$__

Write a fraction for the words. You may draw a picture.

2. three tenths
$\frac{3}{10}$

3. five tenths
$\frac{5}{10}$

4. eight tenths
$\frac{8}{10}$

5. one tenth
$\frac{1}{10}$

6. nine tenths
$\frac{9}{10}$

7. two tenths
$\frac{2}{10}$

8. Daphne answers 10 out of 10 questions on her math quiz correctly. How can she write ten tenths as a fraction?
$\frac{10}{10}$

9. Loren is taking a science test that has 10 parts. She completes half of the test. How many parts of the test does she complete? Explain.

She completes 5 parts. Possible answer: half of 10 parts is 5 parts. 5 out of 10 written as a fraction is $\frac{5}{10}$.

IN76 Response to Intervention • Tier 2

Vocabulary

fraction
denominator
numerator

Name _____

Learn the Math

Althea and Julian flipped a coin 10 times. Julian wrote that six tenths of the flips had an outcome of tails. How can he write six tenths as a fraction?

Vocabulary

fraction
denominator
numerator

Step 1

Shade the tenths model to show six tenths.

Step 2

Write a fraction. Write the number of equal parts in all as the denominator and the number of shaded parts as the numerator.

The **numerator** tells how many parts are being counted. The **denominator** tells how many equal parts are in the whole or in the group.

number of shaded parts $\longrightarrow$ ☐ $\longleftarrow$ numerator

number of equal parts in all $\longrightarrow$ ☐ $\longleftarrow$ denominator

six tenths = _____

So, the fraction _____ represents the number of times the coin landed on tails.

REASONING Althea says the fraction for the number of times the coin landed on heads is $\frac{4}{10}$. Is she correct? Explain.

_____

_____

_____

1. Micah won the 100-meter dash by seven tenths of a second. Write seven tenths as a fraction.

   • Shade the model to show seven tenths.

   • How many equal parts are there in all? _____

   • How many parts are shaded? _____

   • Write seven tenths as a fraction. _____

Write a fraction for the words. You may draw a picture.

2. three tenths

3. five tenths

4. eight tenths

_____

_____

_____

5. one tenth

6. nine tenths

7. two tenths

_____

_____

_____

8. Daphne answers 10 out of 10 questions on her math quiz correctly. How can she write ten tenths as a fraction?

_____

9. Loren is taking a science test that has 10 parts. She completes half of the test. How many parts of the test does she complete? Explain.

_____

_____

Equivalent Fractions for Tenths and Hundredths
Skill 20

Objective
To model and write equivalent fractions for tenths and hundredths

Vocabulary
equivalent fractions Two or more fractions that name the same amount

Materials
decimal models (see *Teacher Resources*)

COMMON ERROR

- Students may shade the same *number of parts* in each model rather than the same *amount* when modeling equivalent fractions.

- To correct this, remind students that equivalent fractions name the same amount. Explain that models should show the same part of the whole shaded.

Learn the Math page IN79 Guide students through Example 1. Point out that both models have the same amount of shading. The tenths model is divided into 10 equal parts and the hundredths model is divided into 100 equal parts.

Discuss the shading of the models in Example 2. Ask: **Do both models have the same amount of shading?** yes **How many parts are shaded in the hundredths model?** 80 **How many parts are shaded in the tenths model?** 8

REASONING Discuss the problem with students. Have students shade models to show that the fractions are equivalent.

Do the Math page IN80 Guide students through Exercise 1. Ask: **How many parts do you shade in the tenths model?** 2 parts **in the hundredths model?** 20 parts **Did you shade the same amount in each model?** yes

Assign Exercises 2–10 and monitor students' work.

Discuss Problem 11. Ask: **How many parts do you shade in the hundredths model?** 90 **How many parts do you shade in the tenths model?** 9

Students who make more than 3 errors in Exercises 1–11 may benefit from the **Alternative Teaching Strategy**.

Alternative Teaching Strategy
Materials: number lines (see *Teacher Resources*)

Give each student a number line ranging from 0–1 with marks on the tenths. Have students label the marks in tenths above the number line and in hundredths beneath the number line. Write the fraction $\frac{3}{10}$ on the board. Ask students to locate the number on the number line. Ask: **What fraction is equivalent to $\frac{3}{10}$?** $\frac{30}{100}$ Repeat with other fractions, alternating between fractions with denominators of 10 and 100.

Equivalent Fractions for Tenths and Hundredths
Skill 20

Learn the Math

You can use what you know about fractions and area models to write equivalent fractions. **Equivalent fractions** are fractions that name the same amount.

Example 1 Complete to show an equivalent fraction.

$\frac{3}{10} = \frac{\boxed{}}{100}$

$\frac{3}{10} = \frac{\boxed{30}}{100}$

Example 2 Complete to show an equivalent fraction.

$\frac{80}{100} = \frac{\boxed{}}{10}$

$\frac{80}{100} = \frac{\boxed{8}}{10}$

REASONING Explain why $\frac{100}{100}$ is equivalent to $\frac{10}{10}$.

Possible answer: both $\frac{100}{100}$ and $\frac{10}{10}$ are equivalent

to 1 whole, or 1.

Do the Math

Skill 20

1. Show an equivalent fraction.

$\frac{2}{10} = \frac{\boxed{}}{100}$

• Shade $\frac{2}{10}$ of the tenths model, and then shade the same amount of the hundredths model.

So, $\frac{2}{10} = \frac{\boxed{20}}{100}$.

Complete to show an equivalent fraction. You may use models to help you complete the exercise.

2. $\frac{9}{10} = \frac{\boxed{90}}{100}$

3. $\frac{40}{100} = \frac{\boxed{4}}{10}$

4. $\frac{50}{100} = \frac{\boxed{5}}{10}$

5. $\frac{1}{10} = \frac{\boxed{10}}{100}$

6. $\frac{6}{10} = \frac{\boxed{60}}{100}$

7. $\frac{70}{100} = \frac{\boxed{7}}{10}$

8. $\frac{100}{100} = \frac{\boxed{10}}{10}$

9. $\frac{\boxed{8}}{10} = \frac{80}{100}$

10. $\frac{30}{100} = \frac{\boxed{3}}{10}$

11. Samuel shades 90 out of 100 equal parts. Write two equivalent fractions to show the amount he shades. Shade the models to show the equivalent fractions.

$\frac{90}{100} = \frac{9}{10}$

Name _____

Learn the Math

You can use what you know about fractions and area models to write equivalent fractions. **Equivalent fractions** are fractions that name the same amount.

Vocabulary

equivalent fractions

Example 1   Complete to show an equivalent fraction.

$\dfrac{3}{10} = \dfrac{\boxed{}}{100}$

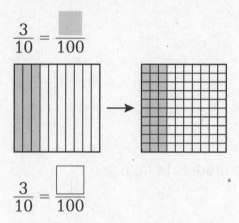

$\dfrac{3}{10} = \dfrac{\boxed{}}{100}$

Example 2   Complete to show an equivalent fraction.

$\dfrac{80}{100} = \dfrac{\boxed{}}{10}$

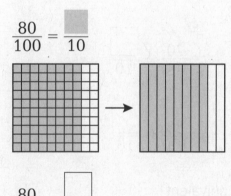

$\dfrac{80}{100} = \dfrac{\boxed{}}{10}$

REASONING Explain why $\dfrac{100}{100}$ is equivalent to $\dfrac{10}{10}$.

_____

_____

_____

1. Show an equivalent fraction.

$$\frac{2}{10} = \frac{\boxed{}}{100}$$

- Shade $\frac{2}{10}$ of the tenths model, and then shade the same amount of the hundredths model.

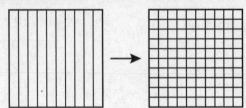

So, $\frac{2}{10} = \frac{\boxed{}}{100}$.

Complete to show an equivalent fraction. You may use models to help you complete the exercise.

2. $\frac{9}{10} = \frac{\boxed{}}{100}$

3. $\frac{40}{100} = \frac{\boxed{}}{10}$

4. $\frac{50}{100} = \frac{\boxed{}}{10}$

5. $\frac{1}{10} = \frac{\boxed{}}{100}$

6. $\frac{6}{10} = \frac{\boxed{}}{100}$

7. $\frac{70}{100} = \frac{\boxed{}}{10}$

8. $\frac{100}{100} = \frac{\boxed{}}{10}$

9. $\frac{\boxed{}}{10} = \frac{80}{100}$

10. $\frac{30}{100} = \frac{\boxed{}}{10}$

11. Samuel shades 90 out of 100 equal parts. Write two equivalent fractions to show the amount he shades. Shade the models to show the equivalent fractions.

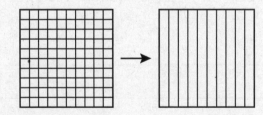

_____

Objective

To relate equivalent fractions and decimals

Vocabulary

decimal A number with one or more digits to the right of the decimal point

decimal point A symbol used to separate the ones and the tenths places in decimals, and to separate dollars from cents in money amounts

tenth One of 10 equal parts of one whole

hundredth One of 100 equal parts of one whole

COMMON ERROR

- When writing a fraction as a decimal, students may write the numerator and denominator after the decimal point.

- To correct this, have students use a model to see the relationship between the number of parts shaded and the total number of equal parts.

Learn the Math page IN83 Read Example 1 aloud. Direct students to look at the model. Ask: **How many equal parts does the model have?** 10 parts **How many parts in the model do you shade?** 5 parts Show students that $\frac{5}{10}$ written as a decimal is 0.5.

Read Example 2 aloud. Ask: **How many parts in the model do you shade?** 75 parts Have students shade 75 squares in the model. Ask: **What fraction represents 75 out of 100?** $\frac{75}{100}$

REASONING Elicit that the model Cayden shades shows both 75 out of 100 parts, and 3 out of 4 parts. Guide students to write both fractions, $\frac{75}{100}$ and $\frac{3}{4}$.

Do the Math page IN84 Read and discuss Exercise 1 with students. Ask: **How many parts in the model do you need to shade?** 8 parts Instruct students to shade the model. Guide them through writing the fraction represented by the model.

Assign Exercises 2–13 and monitor students' work. Check that students know how to write $\frac{1}{100}$ as 0.01, and vice versa. Discuss Problem 14. Have students count the number of shaded parts in the model. Ask: **How many parts out of the 10 equal parts are shaded?** 9 parts **How do you write this as a fraction?** $\frac{9}{10}$ **As a decimal?** 0.9

Students who make more than 4 errors in Exercises 1–14 may benefit from the **Alternative Teaching Strategy**.

Alternative Teaching Strategy

Materials: number lines (See *Teacher Resources*)

Give each student a number line that is divided into hundredths, with tenths labeled as fractions and as decimals. Write the fraction $\frac{3}{10}$ on the board. Have students locate the fraction on their number lines. Ask: **What decimal is equivalent to the fraction $\frac{3}{10}$?** 0.3 Write the decimal 0.25 on the board. Have students locate the decimal on their number lines. Ask: **What fraction is equivalent to 0.25?** $\frac{25}{100}$ Repeat the activity with similar fractions and decimals.

Name _____

Learn the Math

You can use what you know about equivalent fractions to rename a fraction as a decimal.

Vocabulary

decimal
decimal point
tenth
hundredth

Example 1

Shelby runs $\frac{5}{10}$ mile each day during gym class. How can she write the distance that she runs as a decimal?

Shade $\frac{5}{10}$ of the model.

    $\frac{5}{10} = \underline{0.5}$

So, Shelby runs $\underline{0.5}$ mile each day.

Example 2

Cayden runs 0.75 mile each day in gym class. How can he write the distance that he runs as a fraction?

Shade the model to show 0.75.

    75 out of 100 = $\frac{75}{100}$

So, Cayden runs $\frac{75}{100}$ mile each day.

REASONING Cayden shades this model to show the distance that he runs each day. How does this model show two fractions equivalent to 0.75?

Possible answer: this model shows 75 parts shaded out of 100. It is also divided into fourths and shows 3 parts shaded out of 4. So, I can write the fractions $\frac{75}{100}$ and $\frac{3}{4}$ for the model.

Response to Intervention • Tier 2 **IN83**

---

1. Mrs. Rao walked 0.8 mile on Monday. Write the distance that she walked as a fraction.

• Shade the model to show 0.8.

• $\underline{8}$ out of 10 = $\frac{8}{10}$

So, Mrs. Rao walked $\frac{8}{10}$ mile.

Remember
• To rename a fraction as a decimal, write the number of tenths or hundredths after the decimal point.
• To rename a decimal as a fraction, use a model and count the number of shaded parts.

Write as a decimal.

2. $\frac{3}{10}$ $\underline{0.3}$ 3. $\frac{7}{100}$ $\underline{0.07}$

4. $\frac{25}{100}$ $\underline{0.25}$ 5. $\frac{4}{10}$ $\underline{0.4}$

6. $\frac{50}{100}$ $\underline{0.50}$ 7. $\frac{15}{100}$ $\underline{0.15}$

Write as a fraction.

8. 0.38 $\frac{38}{100}$ 9. 0.74 $\frac{74}{100}$

10. 0.6 $\frac{6}{10}$ 11. 0.97 $\frac{97}{100}$

12. 0.50 $\frac{50}{100}$ 13. 0.02 $\frac{2}{100}$

14. The shaded parts of the model show how many miles Fran lives from school. How can she write the distance as a fraction and as a decimal?

Fraction: $\frac{9}{10}$ mile
Decimal: $\underline{0.9}$ mile

IN84 Response to Intervention • Tier 2

Name _____

Learn the Math

You can use what you know about equivalent fractions to rename a fraction as a decimal.

Vocabulary

decimal
decimal point
tenth
hundredth

Example 1

Shelby runs $\frac{5}{10}$ mile each day during gym class. How can she write the distance that she runs as a decimal?

Shade $\frac{5}{10}$ of the model.

$\frac{5}{10}$ = _____

So, Shelby runs _____ mile each day.

Example 2

Cayden runs 0.75 mile each day in gym class. How can he write the distance that he runs as a fraction?

Shade the model to show 0.75.

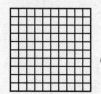

75 out of 100 = $\frac{\square}{100}$

So, Cayden runs _____ mile each day.

REASONING Cayden shades this model to show the distance that he runs each day. How does this model show two fractions equivalent to 0.75?

_____

_____

_____

1. Mrs. Rao walked 0.8 mile on Monday. Write the distance that she walked as a fraction.

   • Shade the model to show 0.8.

   • _____ out of 10 = _____

   So, Mrs. Rao walked _____ mile.

Write as a decimal.

2. $\frac{3}{10}$ _____

3. $\frac{7}{100}$ _____

4. $\frac{25}{100}$ _____

5. $\frac{4}{10}$ _____

6. $\frac{50}{100}$ _____

7. $\frac{15}{100}$ _____

Write as a fraction.

8. 0.38 _____

9. 0.74 _____

10. 0.6 _____

11. 0.97 _____

12. 0.50 _____

13. 0.02 _____

14. The shaded parts of the model show how many miles Fran lives from school. How can she write the distance as a fraction and as a decimal?

   Fraction: _____ mile

   Decimal: _____ mile

Elapsed Time
Skill 22

Objective
To find elapsed time to the nearest 5 minutes

Vocabulary
elapsed time The amount of time that passes from the start of an activity to the end of an activity

COMMON ERROR

- Students may forget to write the hours in the answer.

- To correct this, have students record the number of hours before they calculate the number of minutes.

Learn the Math page IN87 Read the introductory text and Example 1 with students. Review how to tell time on an analog clock. Ask: **What is the start time?** 6:30 P.M. **What time is it one hour later?** 7:30 P.M. Have students trace the jumps in Step 2 as they skip count by fives to count the minutes. **How long does the movie last?** 1 hour 25 minutes Direct students to Example 2 and show how to use a time line to find elapsed time. Ask: **Why does the time line begin at 9:45?** It's the start time. Guide students to record 10:45, then to count on by 15 minutes to 11:00 and by 5-minute intervals to the end time. After students find the elapsed time, discuss similarities between making jumps on the analog clock and on the number line.

REASONING Discuss the question with students. Ask: **Suppose you go to the park** at 2 P.M. and leave 2 hours later. **How can you find what time you leave the park?** Possible answer: start at 2 P.M. and count on 2 hours: 3 P.M., 4 P.M. So, I leave the park at 4 P.M.

Do the Math page IN88 Read and discuss Exercise 1 with students. Ask: **How long is it from 3:15 P.M. to 4:15 P.M.?** 1 hour **How long is it from 4:15 P.M. to 4:25 P.M.?** 10 minutes **How long does Michael ride his skateboard?** 1 hour 10 minutes

Assign Exercises 2–5 and monitor students' work.

Discuss Problem 6 with the students. Have students use a time line or an analog clock to count on 45 minutes from 4:30 P.M.

Students who make more than 1 error in Exercises 1–6 may benefit from the **Alternative Teaching Strategy**.

Alternative Teaching Strategy
Materials: number lines (see *Teacher Resources*)

Help students label a blank number line from 8 A.M. to 5 P.M. to create a time line. Present problem situations students can solve by making jumps on their time lines. Start with hour jumps and then move on to problems involving hours and minutes in 5-minute intervals.

Check that students are counting and recording the hours and minutes correctly before proceeding to a new problem.

Remind students not to count the beginning time as the first hour.

Name _____

Learn the Math

Elapsed time is the amount of time that passes from the start of an activity to the end of the activity. You can use a clock or a time line to help you find elapsed time.

Vocabulary

elapsed time

Example 1

Kian and his friends go to a movie. The movie begins at 6:30 P.M. and ends at 7:55 P.M. How long does the movie last?

| **Step 1**
Start at 6:30. Count the hours on the clock.
<u>1</u> hour | | **Step 2**
Skip count by fives to count the minutes.
<u>25</u> minutes | |

So, the movie lasts <u>1</u> hour <u>25</u> minutes.

Example 2

Use a time line. How much time elapses from 9:45 A.M. to 11:10 A.M.?

| **Step 1**
Find 9:45 on the time line. Count on from 9:45 to 11:10. Show the time on the time line. | **Step 2**
Draw jumps on the time line. Add to find the total hours and minutes. |

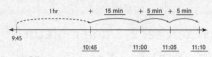

So, <u>1</u> hour <u>25</u> minutes elapse from 9:45 A.M. to 11:10 A.M.

REASONING If you know the start time and the elapsed time, how can you find the end time?
Possible answer: count the amount of elapsed time from the start time. You'll end at the end time.

Response to Intervention • Tier 2 **IN87**

Do the Math

1. Michael rides his skateboard from 3:15 P.M. to 4:25 P.M. How long does Michael ride his skateboard?

Remember
Do not count the beginning time as the first hour.

- What is the start time? <u>3:15</u> P.M.
- Count on from <u>3:15 P.M.</u> to <u>4:25 P.M.</u> on the time line.

- From 3:15 P.M. to 4:15 P.M. is <u>1</u> hour.
- From 4:15 P.M. to 4:25 P.M. is <u>10</u> minutes.

So, Michael rides his skateboard for <u>1</u> hour <u>10</u> minutes.

Find the elapsed time. **Possible drawings are shown for 4 and 5.**

| 2. Start: 12:20 P.M.
End: 2:20 P.M.

<u>2 hours</u> | 3. Start: 8:30 A.M.
End: 9:40 A.M.
<u>1 hour 10 minutes</u> |
| 4. Start: 4:45 P.M. End: 5:20 P.M.
<u>35 minutes</u> | 5. Start: 6:05 P.M. End: 8:35 P.M.
<u>2 hours 30 minutes</u> |

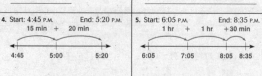

6. Karina begins her piano lesson at 4:30 P.M. Her lesson lasts for 45 minutes. What time does her lesson end? <u>5:15</u> P.M.

IN88 Response to Intervention • Tier 2

IN86 Response to Intervention • Tier 2

© Houghton Mifflin Harcourt Publishing Company

Name _____

Learn the Math

Elapsed time is the amount of time that passes from the start of an activity to the end of the activity. You can use a clock or a time line to help you find elapsed time.

Vocabulary

elapsed time

Example 1

Kian and his friends go to a movie. The movie begins at 6:30 P.M. and ends at 7:55 P.M. How long does the movie last?

Step 1		Step 2	
Start at 6:30. Count the hours on the clock. ___ hour		Skip count by fives to count the minutes. ___ minutes	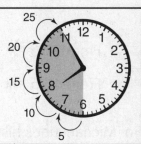

So, the movie lasts ___ hour ___ minutes.

Example 2

Use a time line. How much time elapses from 9:45 A.M. to 11:10 A.M.?

Step 1	Step 2
Find 9:45 on the time line. Count on from 9:45 to 11:10. Show the time on the time line.	Draw jumps on the time line. Add to find the total hours and minutes.

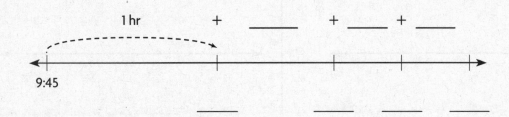

So, ___ hour ___ minutes elapse from 9:45 A.M. to 11:10 A.M.

REASONING If you know the start time and the elapsed time, how can you find the end time?

_____

_____

© Houghton Mifflin Harcourt Publishing Company

1. Michael rides his skateboard from 3:15 P.M. to 4:25 P.M. How long does Michael ride his skateboard?

Remember

Do not count the beginning time as the first hour.

   • What is the start time? _____

   • Count on from _____ to _____ on the time line.

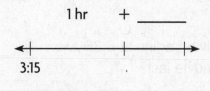

   1 hr   + _____

   3:15

   ___ ___

   • From 3:15 P.M. to 4:15 P.M. is ____ hour.

   • From 4:15 P.M. to 4:25 P.M. is ____ minutes.

So, Michael rides his skateboard for ____ hour ____ minutes.

Find the elapsed time.

2. Start: 12:20 P.M.
   End: 2:20 P.M.

_____

3. Start: 8:30 A.M.
   End: 9:40 A.M.

_____

4. Start: 4:45 P.M.   End: 5:20 P.M.

_____

5. Start: 6:05 P.M.   End: 8:35 P.M.

_____

6. Karina begins her piano lesson at 4:30 P.M. Her lesson lasts for 45 minutes. What time does her lesson end? _____

Objective

To use basic facts and patterns to multiply multiples of 10, 100, and 1,000

COMMON ERROR

- Students may forget to write the additional zero in the final product when the basic fact has a zero in the product.

- To correct this, have students use patterns and underline the zeros in the patterns when multiplying or dividing multiples of 10, 100, and 1,000.

Learn the Math page IN91 Discuss Example 1 with students. Explain that students can use a basic fact and patterns to find products. Ask: **What basic fact can you use to find 11 × 100?** 11 × 1

Remind students that the final product has the same number of zeros as the factors, unless the basic fact has a zero in the product. Explain that in such cases the final product will have an additional zero.

Discuss Example 2 with students. Point out that they can use basic facts and patterns to answer this question also. Ask: **What basic fact can you use to find 8 × 200?** 8 × 2

REASONING Discuss the problem with students. Suggest students use a multiplication pattern to help. Ask: **How many zeros will the product of 400 and 500 have? Why?** Possible answer: the product will have 5 zeros, the 4 zeros in the factors and the zero in the product of

the basic fact. 4 × 5 = 20, so 4<u>00</u> × 5<u>00</u> = 200,000.

Do the Math page IN92 Read and discuss Exercises 1 and 2 with students. Guide students to solve the problems. Help students identify the basic fact to use to solve each problem.

Assign Exercises 3–6 and monitor students' work.

Discuss Problems 7 and 8 with the students. For Problem 7, ask: **What basic fact can you use to solve the problem?** 6 × 10 For Problem 8, guide students in counting the number of zeros in the factors.

Students who make more than 2 errors in Exercises 1–8 may benefit from the **Alternative Teaching Strategy**.

Alternative Teaching Strategy

Manipulatives and Materials: so[..] tiles, 1-inch grid paper (see *Teacher [..]ources*)

Write a problem on the boa[..] [..]uch as 1,000 × 4. Have student[..] [..]py the problem onto grid paper, wr[..]ting one digit in each square. Then have students use their tiles to cover each zero so that only the basic fact is showing. Students should write and solve the basic fact below the original problem: 1 × 4 = 4. Next, have students count how many tiles they used to cover the zeros. Tell students to write a zero at the end of the product of the basic fact for each tile they used: 4000. Help students make the connection between the number of tiles they use and the number of zeros to write at the end of the product. Remind students to write a comma after the thousands digit: 4,000. Repeat for different examples.

Learn the Math

You can use basic facts and patterns to multiply multiples of 10, 100, and 1,000 mentally.

Example 1

Mrs. Wong drives 100 miles to and from work each month. How many miles will Mrs. Wong drive to and from work in 11 months?

Multiply 11 × 100.

Multiplication can be thought of as repeated addition.

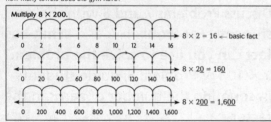

$11 \times 1 = 11$ ← basic fact

$11 \times 1\underline{0} = 11\underline{0}$

$11 \times 1\underline{00} = 1,1\underline{00}$

So, Mrs. Wong will drive 1,100 miles to and from work in 11 months.

Example 2

A gym has 8 packs of towels. If there are 200 towels in each pack, how many towels does the gym have?

Multiply 8 × 200.

$8 \times 2 = 16$ ← basic fact

$8 \times 2\underline{0} = 16\underline{0}$

$8 \times 2\underline{00} = 1,6\underline{00}$

So, the gym has 1,600 towels.

REASONING If you multiply 400 × 500, how many zeros will the product have?

Possible answer: 5 zeros; 400 × 500 = 200,000

Do the Math

Solve. Use basic facts and patterns to help you.

> **Remember**
> • The number of zeros in the product increases as the number of zeros in a factor increases.

1.

• What basic fact does this number line show?

$\underline{10} \times \underline{2} = \underline{20}$

• Use the basic fact to find

$10 \times 20 = \underline{200}$ and $10 \times 200 = \underline{2,000}$

2.

• What basic fact does this number line show?

$\underline{4} \times \underline{8} = \underline{32}$

• Use the basic fact to find

$40 \times 8 = \underline{320}$ and $4,000 \times 8 = \underline{32,000}$

Use a pattern to find each product or quotient.

3. $3 \times 10 = \underline{30}$
$3 \times 100 = \underline{300}$
$3 \times 1,000 = \underline{3,000}$

4. $7 \times 10 = \underline{70}$
$7 \times 100 = \underline{700}$
$7 \times 1,000 = \underline{7,000}$

5. $21 \times 10 = \underline{210}$
$21 \times 100 = \underline{2,100}$
$21 \times 1,000 = \underline{21,000}$

6. $38 \times 10 = \underline{380}$
$38 \times 100 = \underline{3,800}$
$38 \times 1,000 = \underline{38,000}$

7. The school bought 60 cases of reusable water bottles for a school picnic. Each case contains 10 bottles. How many water bottles did the school buy?

$60 \times 10 = 600;\ 600$ **water bottles**

8. Explain why 15 × 10 has one zero in the product while 20 × 10 has two zeros in the product.

Possible answer: in 15 × 10 = 150, one factor has a zero. In 20 × 10 = 200, both factors have a zero.

Name _____

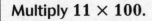

You can use basic facts and patterns to multiply
multiples of 10, 100, and 1,000 mentally.

Example 1
Mrs. Wong drives 100 miles to and from work each month. How
many miles will Mrs. Wong drive to and from work in 11 months?

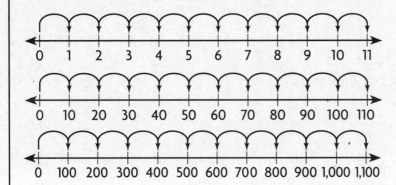

Multiply 11 × 100.

Multiplication can be thought of as repeated addition.

$11 \times 1 = 11$ ← basic fact

$11 \times 1\underline{0} = 11\underline{0}$

$11 \times 1\underline{00} = 1,1\underline{00}$

So, Mrs. Wong will drive _____ miles to and from work in 11 months.

Example 2
A gym has 8 packs of towels. If there are 200 towels in each pack,
how many towels does the gym have?

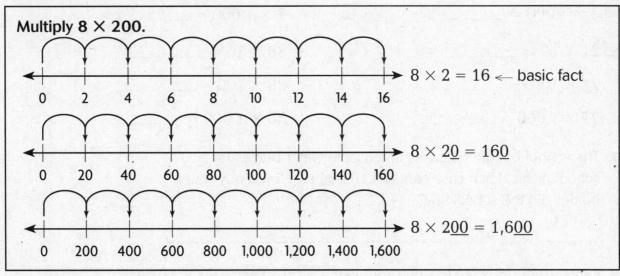

Multiply 8 × 200.

$8 \times 2 = 16$ ← basic fact

$8 \times 2\underline{0} = 16\underline{0}$

$8 \times 2\underline{00} = 1,6\underline{00}$

So, the gym has 1,600 towels.

REASONING If you multiply 400 × 500, how many zeros will the product have?

© Houghton Mifflin Harcourt Publishing Company

Solve. Use basic facts and patterns to help you.

1.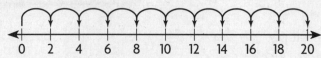

   • What basic fact does this number line show?

   _____ × _____ = _____.

   • Use the basic fact to find

   $10 \times 20 =$ _____ and $10 \times 200 =$ _____.

Remember

• The number of zeros in the product increases as the number of zeros in a factor increases.

2.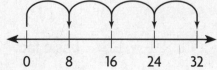

   • What basic fact does this number line show?

   _____ × _____ = _____

   • Use the basic fact to find

   $40 \times 8 =$ _____ and $4{,}000 \times 8 =$ _____.

Use a pattern to find each product or quotient.

3. $3 \times 10 =$ _____

   $3 \times 100 =$ _____

   $3 \times 1{,}000 =$ _____

5. $21 \times 10 =$ _____

   $21 \times 100 =$ _____

   $21 \times 1{,}000 =$ _____

4. $7 \times 10 =$ _____

   $7 \times 100 =$ _____

   $7 \times 1{,}000 =$ _____

6. $38 \times 10 =$ _____

   $38 \times 100 =$ _____

   $38 \times 1{,}000 =$ _____

7. The school bought 60 cases of reusable water bottles for a school picnic. Each case contains 10 bottles. How many water bottles did the school buy?

   _____

8. Explain why 15×10 has one zero in the product while 20×10 has two zeros in the product.

   _____

   _____

Congruent Shapes
Skill 24

Objective
To identify two-dimensional congruent shapes

Vocabulary
congruent Shapes that have the same size and shape

COMMON ERROR

- Students may incorrectly identify shapes as being not congruent when the shapes are in different positions.

- To correct this, have students use tracing paper to copy one of the shapes. The position of the traced shape can be reoriented to more easily compare it to the other shape.

Learn the Math page IN95 Discuss the definition of *congruent* with students. Direct them to the two pairs of congruent shapes. Have students count the length and the width of each rectangle to verify that the shapes are the same size. To emphasize that shapes do not need to be in the same position to be congruent, have students trace the triangle on the left on another sheet of paper, turn the tracing, and then place the traced triangle on top of the triangle on the right.

Direct students to the pairs of shapes that are not congruent. Discuss that the shapes in the first pair are the same size but are not the same shape and that the shapes in the second pair are the same shape but are not the same size.

REASONING Discuss the question with students. Students may wish to trace one triangle and place the tracing over the

other triangles to compare the size and shape. Remind them that they can rotate their tracing. They can also count the lengths of the sides of each triangle to verify that the triangles are congruent.

Do the Math page IN96 Discuss Exercise 1 with students. Ask: **How can you determine whether the shapes are congruent?** Possible answer: I can trace one triangle and compare it to the size and shape of the other triangle. **Are the two shapes congruent?** yes

Assign Exercises 2–7 and monitor students' work. Encourage students to rotate the page to view the figures from different orientations. This will reinforce the idea that the figures do not need to have the same position in order to be congruent.

Discuss Problem 8 with students. Have them lay one page of their book on top of another to see that the pages are the same size and shape and are, therefore, congruent.

Students who make more than 2 errors in Exercises 1–8 may benefit from the **Alternative Teaching Strategy**.

Alternative Teaching Strategy
Manipulatives: pattern blocks

Have students select a pattern block and trace it on a sheet of paper. Ask them to trace the same pattern block on another sheet of paper. Ask: **Are the two shapes congruent?** yes **How do you know?** They are the same size and same shape. If students have difficulty identifying the shapes as congruent, have them place one drawing on top of the other and line up the traced shapes. Repeat with other pattern blocks. Encourage students to rotate each block before tracing it the second time.

Name _____

Learn the Math

Shapes that have the same size and the same shape are **congruent**.

The shapes in each of these pairs are congruent. They have the same size and the same shape.

Vocabulary

congruent

The shapes in each of these pairs are not congruent.

These have the same size, but are not the same shape.

These have the same shape, but are not the same size.

REASONING Ian says all the figures below are congruent. Is he correct? Explain.

Yes; possible answer: the triangles are in different positions, but they are still the same size and the same shape.

Response to Intervention • Tier 2 **IN95**

Do the Math

Skill 24

1. Lola draws the two shapes below. Are they congruent?

Remember

If the shapes are the same size and the same shape, they are congruent.

• Do the shapes have the same size? **yes**
• Do they have the same shape? **yes**

Since position of the shapes does not matter, are the shapes congruent? **yes**

Write whether the two shapes are congruent. Write yes or no.

2. **yes**

3. **no**

4. **yes**

5. **yes**

6. **no**

7. **yes**

8. **REASONING** Are the pages of your math book congruent? Explain.
Yes; possible answer: each page in a book is the same size and the same shape.

IN96 Response to Intervention • Tier 2

Name _____

Learn the Math

Shapes that have the same size and the same shape are **congruent**.

Vocabulary

congruent

The shapes in each of these pairs are congruent. They have the same size and the same shape.

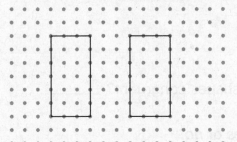   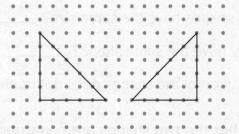

The shapes in each of these pairs are not congruent.

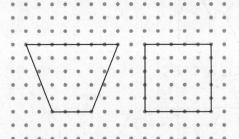   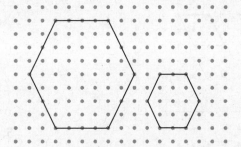

These have the same size, but are not the same shape.

These have the same shape, but are not the same size.

REASONING Ian says all the figures below are congruent. Is he correct? Explain.

_____

_____

_____

1. Lola draws the two shapes below.
   Are they congruent?

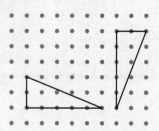

• Do the shapes have the same size? _____

• Do they have the same shape? _____

Since position of the shapes does not matter, are the shapes congruent? _____

Write whether the two shapes are congruent. Write *yes* or *no*.

2.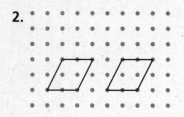

_____

3.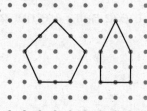

_____

4.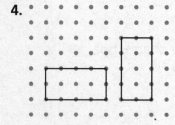

_____

5.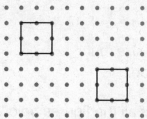

_____

6.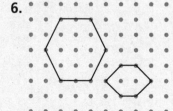

_____

7.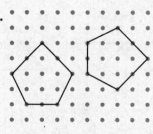

_____

8. **REASONING** Are the pages of your math book congruent? Explain.

_____

_____

Patterns
Skill 25

Objective
To identify, describe, and extend repeating patterns

Vocabulary
pattern unit The part of a pattern that repeats

repeating pattern A pattern that uses the same pattern unit over and over again

COMMON ERROR

- Students may have difficulty identifying the pattern unit.

- To correct this, have them say the names of the shapes or objects out loud. The rhythm of the words can help identify the pattern unit.

Learn the Math page IN99 Guide students through Example 1. Help students identify the pattern unit. Ask: **What is the pattern unit?** triangle, square **How can you decide what comes next?** Possible answer: since I know the pattern unit, I know that the next two shapes will be triangle, square.

When discussing Example 2, point out that pattern units can be made up of all different shapes, or that some shapes can repeat within the pattern unit. Ask: **Which shape repeats in this pattern unit?** circle **What is the pattern unit?** rectangle, circle, circle

Read the question aloud to students. Ask: **What if there were a square between each pair of circles? How would this change the pattern unit?** Possible answer: the pattern unit would be rectangle, circle, square, circle. If students have difficulty identifying

the new pattern unit, ask for a volunteer to draw the new pattern on the board.

REASONING If students do not recognize the pattern unit, have them draw the pattern.

Do the Math page IN100 Guide students through Exercise 1. Ask: **What is the pattern unit?** circle, square **How many shapes are in the pattern unit?** two **Where do you look to decide which shape comes next?** the last shape in the pattern

Assign Exercises 2–7 and monitor students' work.

Discuss Problem 8 with students. Encourage them to say the names of the shapes on each bookmark to help them identify the bookmark with the repeating pattern.

Students who make more than 2 errors in Exercises 1–8 may benefit from the **Alternative Teaching Strategy**.

Alternative Teaching Strategy
Manipulatives: pattern blocks

Arrange students in pairs and give each student a set of pattern blocks. Draw the repeating pattern *triangle*, *square*, *triangle*, *square*, *triangle*, *square* on the board. Have pairs model this pattern using their pattern blocks. Ask: **What is the pattern unit?** triangle, square Have students model the next two shapes in the pattern. Next ask one student in the pair to describe a different repeating pattern that can be formed with the blocks. Have the other student model the pattern with the pattern blocks. Both students should record the pattern made. Repeat the activity. Have students alternate tasks. Encourage students to create patterns that have more than two shapes in the pattern unit.

Learn the Math

The part of the pattern that repeats is the **pattern unit**.

When the same pattern unit is used over and over again, it makes a **repeating pattern**.

Vocabulary

pattern unit
repeating pattern

Example 1

Draw the next two shapes in the pattern below.

△ ☐ △ ☐ △ ☐ △ ☐ △ ☐

This pattern unit is ___triangle, square___

So, the next two shapes in the pattern are: *triangle, square*.

Example 2

Draw the pattern unit for the pattern below.

☐ ○ ○ ☐ ○ ○ ☐ ○ ○

☐ ○ ○

What if there were a square between each pair of circles?
Draw what the pattern unit would look like.

☐ ○ ☐ ○

REASONING In music class, Mr. Thomas lines up students by the instruments they play: tuba, drum, tuba, drum, tuba, drum, tuba. What is the pattern unit? Will tuba or drum come next? How do you know?

The pattern unit is tuba, drum. Drum will come next.

Possible answer: since tuba was the last item in the

pattern, drum will come next.

Do the Math

1. Circle the pattern unit. Describe the pattern. Then draw the next two shapes.

- The pattern unit is ___circle___ ___square___
  ___Circle___ , ___square___ come next.

○ ◇ ○ ◇ ○ ◇ ○ ◇

Remember
The pattern unit is the part of the pattern that repeats.

Draw the next shapes in the pattern.

2. ▽ △ ▽ △ ▽ △ ▽ △

3. ◁ ◁ ◁ ◁ ◁ ◁ ◁ ◁

4. ○ ◁ ○ ◁ ○ ◁ ○ ◁

5. ☐ ○ ☐ ☐ ○ ☐ ☐ ○ ☐ ○ ☐

6. ◁ ❘ ◁ ◁ ❘ ◁ ◁ ❘ ◁ ❘ ◁

7. ⬠ ○ ❘ ⬠ ○ ❘ ⬠ ○ ❘ ⬠ ○ ❘

8. Circle the bookmark with the repeating pattern. Describe the pattern unit.

___square, circle___

o ☐ ○ ☐ ○ ☐ ○

o ☐ ○ ☐ ○ ☐ ◁

Name _____

Learn the Math

The part of the pattern that repeats is the **pattern unit**.

When the same pattern unit is used over and over again, it makes a **repeating pattern.**

Vocabulary

pattern unit
repeating pattern

Example 1

Draw the next two shapes in the pattern below.

This pattern unit is _____.

So, the next two shapes in the pattern are: *triangle*, *square*.

Example 2

Draw the pattern unit for the pattern below.

What if there were a square between each pair of circles?
Draw what the pattern unit would look like.

REASONING In music class, Mr. Thomas lines up students by the instruments they play: tuba, drum, tuba, drum, tuba, drum, tuba. What is the pattern unit? Will tuba or drum come next? How do you know?

_____

_____

_____

1. Circle the pattern unit. Describe the pattern. Then draw the next two shapes.

- The pattern unit is _____, _____.

- _____, _____ come next.

○ ◇ ○ ◇ ○ ◇ __ __

Draw the next shapes in the pattern.

2. ▽ △ ▽ △ ▽ △ __ __

3. ◿ ◺ ◿ ◺ ◿ ◺ ◿ ◺ __ __ __

4. ○ ◺ ○ ◺ ○ ◺ __ __

5. ▢ ○ ▢ ▢ ○ ▢ ▢ ○ ▢ __ __ __ __

6. ⏢ ▯ ◿ ⏢ ▯ ◿ ⏢ ▯ ◿ __ __ __ __

7. ⌂ ○ ▯ ⌂ ○ ▯ ⌂ ○ ▯ __ __ __

8. Circle the bookmark with the repeating pattern. Describe the pattern unit.

_____

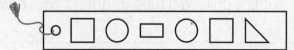

Objective

To add whole numbers using up to four addends

Vocabulary

addend Any of the numbers that are added in addition

sum The answer to an addition problem

COMMON ERROR

- When using place value to add, students may forget to add the regrouped ones, tens, or hundreds.

- To correct this, encourage students to write addition problems in place-value charts and write the regrouped numbers over the correct columns.

Learn the Math page IN103 Guide students through Example 1. Discuss that breaking apart the addends results in numbers that are easy to add mentally. Ask: **What is the sum of all the place-value positions?** 370 Remind students to compare their answers to their estimates.

Guide students through Example 2. Assist them as they record the regrouping and the sum.

REASONING Ask: **What did Tim forget to do?** He forgot to regroup 12 ones as 1 ten 2 ones and then add the regrouped ten. Remind students to record regrouped digits when they are adding.

Do the Math page IN104 Have a student read Exercise 1 aloud. Ask: **What**

do you need to find? the number of miles the Engels will drive in all Guide students to break apart each addend, to find the sum of each place-value position, and then to add the sums of the place values.

Assign Exercises 2–11 and monitor students' work. Encourage students to rewrite the problems in a vertical format to find each sum.

Discuss Problem 12. Have students write a vertical addition problem to find the sum. Ask: **What are the addends?** 48, 201, 233, and 427 Ask volunteers to show on the board how to find the sum by using the break-apart strategy and by using place value.

Students who make more than 3 errors in Exercises 1–12 may benefit from the **Alternative Teaching Strategy**.

Alternative Teaching Strategy

Manipulatives: base-ten blocks

Write the addition problem 45 + 26 + 323 on the board. Instruct students to write the problem in vertical format and to model each addend using base-ten blocks. Say: **Add the ones.** Ask: **How many ones do you have?** 14 ones **Do you need to regroup?** yes Have students model regrouping by trading 10 small cubes for 1 long. Then have students record the ones and the regrouped ten. Say: **Add the tens.** Ask: **How many tens do you have?** 9 tens Have students record 9 tens. **Do you need to regroup?** no Say: **Add the hundreds.** Ask: **How many hundreds do you have?** 3 hundreds Have students record the hundreds. Ask: **What is the sum?** 394 Repeat this activity for similar problems with three or four addends.

Learn the Math

Kevin, Julia, Li, and Tyler collect baseball cards. Kevin has 118 cards, Tyler has 102 cards, Julia has 83 cards, and Li has 67 cards. How many cards do they have altogether?

Vocabulary

addend

sum

Example 1 Use a break-apart strategy.

Add. $118 + 102 + 83 + 67$ Estimate. $100 + 100 + 80 + 70 = \underline{350}$

Break apart the addends.

Start with the hundreds place. Add each place.

$$
\begin{array}{r}
118 \rightarrow 100 + 10 + 8 \\
102 \rightarrow 100 + 0 + 2 \\
83 \rightarrow 80 + 3 \\
+67 \rightarrow 60 7 \\
\hline
200 + \underline{150} + \underline{20}
\end{array}
$$ Add to find the sum. $\underline{370}$

So, they have $\underline{370}$ baseball cards altogether.

Example 2 Use place value.

Add. $642 + 54 + 9$ Estimate. $600 + 50 + 10 = \underline{660}$

Step 1	Step 2	Step 3
Add the ones.	Add the tens.	Add the hundreds.
Regroup.	Regroup.	
15 ones = 1 ten $\underline{5}$ ones	10 tens = $\underline{1}$ hundred 0 tens	
$\boxed{1}$	$\boxed{1}_1$	$\begin{array}{r} 1\,1 \\ 642 \\ 54 \\ +9 \\ \hline \boxed{7}05 \end{array}$
$\begin{array}{r}642 \\ 54 \\ +9 \\ \hline \boxed{5}\end{array}$	$\begin{array}{r}642 \\ 54 \\ +9 \\ \hline \boxed{0}5\end{array}$	

So, $642 + 54 + 9 = \underline{705}$.

REASONING Tim says that $54 + 83 + 15 = 142$. Is he correct? Explain.

No, $54 + 83 + 15 = 152$; possible answer: Tim forgot to regroup the ones as 1 ten 2 ones.

Do the Math

Skill **26**

1. The Engels are planning a trip from Orlando, FL, to Washington, D.C. They plan to stop two nights along the way. The first day they will drive 269 miles, the second day they will drive 291 miles, and the last day they will drive 314 miles. How many miles will they drive in all?

Remember
Estimating before you find the exact answer helps you know if your answer is reasonable.

- Estimate. $300 + 300 + 300 = \underline{900}$
- Break apart the addends.

$$
\begin{array}{r}
269 \rightarrow 200 + 60 + \boxed{9} \\
291 \rightarrow 200 + \boxed{90} + \boxed{1} \\
+314 \rightarrow \boxed{300} + \boxed{10} + \boxed{4} \\
\hline
700 + 160 + 14
\end{array}
$$

- Add to find the sum. $700 + 160 + 14 = \underline{874}$

So, the Engels will drive $\underline{874}$ miles.

Estimate. Then find the sum. Check students' estimates.

2. $\begin{array}{r} 29 + 53 + 571 \\ 29 \\ 53 \\ +\,571 \\ \hline 653 \end{array}$ 3. $\begin{array}{r} 725 + 49 + 8 \\ 725 \\ 49 \\ +8 \\ \hline 782 \end{array}$

4. $129 + 315 + 32 = \underline{476}$ 5. $76 + 94 + 545 = \underline{715}$

6. $64 + 9 + 212 + 789 = \underline{1,074}$ 7. $368 + 83 + 226 + 17 = \underline{694}$

8. $194 + 452 + 109 + 67 = \underline{822}$ 9. $52 + 45 + 654 + 486 = \underline{1,237}$

10. $83 + 214 + 76 + 339 = \underline{712}$ 11. $27 + 34 + 98 + 165 = \underline{324}$

12. On the trip home from Washington, D.C., the Engels plan to take a different route to visit friends. The first day they will drive 48 miles, the second day 201 miles, the third day 233 miles, and the last day 427 miles. How many miles will they drive in all?

909 miles

Name _____

Learn the Math

Kevin, Julia, Li, and Tyler collect baseball cards. Kevin has 118 cards, Tyler has 102 cards, Julia has 83 cards, and Li has 67 cards. How many cards do they have altogether?

Vocabulary

addend

sum

Example 1 Use a break-apart strategy.

Add. $118 + 102 + 83 + 67$ Estimate. $100 + 100 + 80 + 70 =$ _____

Break apart the addends.

Start with the hundreds place. Add each place.

$$
\begin{array}{rcl}
118 & \rightarrow & 100 + 10 + 8 \\
102 & \rightarrow & 100 + \ 0 + 2 \\
83 & \rightarrow & \quad\quad 80 + 3 \\
+ \ 67 & \rightarrow & \quad\quad 60 \quad 7 \\
\hline
& & 200 + \text{\_\_\_} + \text{\_\_\_}
\end{array}
$$

Add to find the sum. _____

So, they have _____ baseball cards altogether.

Example 2 Use place value.

Add. $642 + 54 + 9$ Estimate. $600 + 50 + 10 =$ _____

Step 1	Step 2	Step 3
Add the ones.	Add the tens.	Add the hundreds.
Regroup.	Regroup.	
15 ones = 1 ten ____ ones	10 tens = ____ hundred 0 tens	
$\square$ 642 54 + 9 $\square$	$\square_1$ 642 54 + 9 $\square$5	¹¹ 642 54 + 9 $\square$05

So, $642 + 54 + 9 =$ _____.

REASONING Tim says that $54 + 83 + 15 = 142$. Is he correct? Explain.

_____

Do the Math

1. The Engels are planning a trip from Orlando, FL, to Washington, D.C. They plan to stop two nights along the way. The first day they will drive 269 miles, the second day they will drive 291 miles, and the last day they will drive 314 miles. How many miles will they drive in all?

   • Estimate. $300 + 300 + 300 =$ _____

   • Break apart the addends.

$$
\begin{array}{rcl}
269 & \rightarrow & 2\,0\,0 + 6\,0 + \boxed{} \\
291 & \rightarrow & 2\,0\,0 + \boxed{} + \boxed{} \\
+\ 314 & \rightarrow & \boxed{} + \boxed{} + \boxed{} \\
\hline
& & \underline{} + \underline{} + \underline{}
\end{array}
$$

   • Add to find the sum. $700 + 160 + 14 =$ _____

   So, the Engels will drive _____ miles.

Estimate. Then find the sum.

2. $29 + 53 + 571$

$$
\begin{array}{r}
29 \\
53 \\
+\ 571 \\
\hline
\end{array}
$$

3. $725 + 49 + 8$

$$
\begin{array}{r}
725 \\
49 \\
+\ 8 \\
\hline
\end{array}
$$

4. $129 + 315 + 32 =$ _____

5. $76 + 94 + 545 =$ _____

6. $64 + 9 + 212 + 789 =$ _____

7. $368 + 83 + 226 + 17 =$ _____

8. $194 + 452 + 109 + 67 =$ _____

9. $52 + 45 + 654 + 486 =$ _____

10. $83 + 214 + 76 + 339 =$ _____

11. $27 + 34 + 98 + 165 =$ _____

12. On the trip home from Washington, D.C., the Engels plan to take a different route to visit friends. The first day they will drive 48 miles, the second day 201 miles, the third day 233 miles, and the last day 427 miles. How many miles will they drive in all?

   _____

Multiply Whole Numbers

Skill 27

Objective

To multiply 2-digit numbers by 1-digit numbers

Manipulatives and Materials

base-ten blocks, 1-inch grid paper (see *Teacher Resources*)

COMMON ERROR

- Students may write a regrouped number above the incorrect place-value position.

- To correct this, have students write multiplication problems on grid paper. The grid lines will help students align digits when regrouping.

Learn the Math page IN107 Discuss with students different strategies for solving multiplication problems.

Guide students through Example 1. Students can use base-ten blocks to model the problem and to help find the product. Remind students that when they regroup, they need to make sure they write the regrouped digit above the correct place-value position. Have students compare the product to the estimate. Remind them that since 115 is close to 100 the product is reasonable.

Guide students through Example 2. If students have difficulty finding the partial products, have them count the number of shaded squares in each step. Remind students to compare the product to the estimate to check if the product is reasonable.

REASONING Discuss the problem with students. Have them write the problem

vertically and show their work. Ask: **Why is the first partial product 80 instead of 8?** Possible answer: I am multiplying 2×4 tens, not 2×4 ones.

Do the Math page IN108 Discuss Exercise 1 with students. Ask: **What do you need to do to solve this problem?** Find 3×18. Guide students through multiplying the ones and regrouping, and then through multiplying the tens and adding the regrouped tens.

Assign Exercises 2–12 and monitor students' work.

Discuss Problem 13. Ask: **What multiplication problem do you write to find the number of muffins the shop sells in all?** 6×37 Invite student volunteers to show how to find the product using both place-value regrouping and partial products.

Students who make more than 4 errors in Exercises 1–13 may benefit from the **Alternative Teaching Strategy**.

Alternative Teaching Strategy

Manipulatives: two-color counters

Have students use the Distributive Property to break apart factors into numbers that are easy to multiply. Write the problem 7×16 on the board. Have students use counters to model 7 rows of 16 counters. Have them break apart the model to make two smaller groups for the factor 16. Have students break the model between the seventh and eighth columns. Ask: **What two facts are shown by the model?** $7 \times 7 = 49$ and $7 \times 9 = 63$ Instruct students to add the two products to find the product of 7×16. $49 + 63 = 112$ Repeat with similar problems.

Learn the Math

You can multiply using place value and partial products.

Example 1 Use place value with regrouping.
Multiply. 5×23 Estimate. $5 \times 20 = 100$

	Model	Think	Record
Step 1		Multiply the ones. 5×3 ones = __15__ ones	$\begin{array}{r} 1 \\ 23 \\ \times\ 5 \\ \hline 5 \end{array}$ Regroup the 15 ones as 1 ten 5 ones.
Step 2		Multiply the tens. 5×2 tens = __10__ tens. Add the regrouped ten. 10 tens + 1 ten = 11 tens	$\begin{array}{r} 1 \\ 23 \\ \times\ 5 \\ \hline 115 \end{array}$ Regroup 11 tens as 1 hundred 1 ten.

So, $5 \times 23 = $ __115__ .

Example 2 Use partial products.
Multiply. 4×23 Estimate. $4 \times 25 = 100$

	Model	Think	Record
Step 1	20 3	Multiply the tens. 4×2 tens = __8__ tens	$\begin{array}{r} 20 \\ \times\ 4 \\ \hline 80 \end{array}$
Step 2	20 3	Multiply the ones. 4×3 ones = __12__ ones	$\begin{array}{r} 3 \\ \times\ 4 \\ \hline 12 \end{array}$
Step 3	20 3 (80 12)	Add the partial products.	$\begin{array}{r} 23 \\ \times\ 4 \\ \hline 80 \\ +12 \\ \hline 92 \end{array}$

So, $4 \times 23 = $ __92__

REASONING Explain how to find 2×42 using partial products. **Possible answer: multiply the tens, 2×4 tens = 8 tens, or 80. Multiply the ones, 2×2 ones = 4 ones. Then add the partial products, $80 + 4 = 84$.**

Do the Math

Skill 27

1. Mr. Spencer ordered 3 boxes of magnets. Each box has 18 magnets in it. How many magnets does he have in all?

Multiply. 3×18 Estimate. $3 \times 20 = 60$
- Multiply the ones.
  3×8 ones = __24__ ones
  Regroup the ones.   2
- Multiply the tens.
  3×1 ten = __3__ tens
  $\begin{array}{r} 1\ 8 \\ \times\ 3 \\ \hline 5\ 4 \end{array}$
  Add the regrouped tens.
  __3__ tens + 2 tens = __5__ tens

So, Mr. Spencer has __54__ magnets in all.

> **Remember**
> - You can find products using place value with regrouping.
> - You can find products using partial products.

Find the product.

2.
$\begin{array}{r} 23 \\ \times\ 7 \\ \hline \boxed{40} \\ +\boxed{21} \\ \hline \boxed{161} \end{array}$
| 20 | 3 |
| 7 | |

3.
$\begin{array}{r} \boxed{1} \\ 26 \\ \times\ 3 \\ \hline \boxed{78} \end{array}$

4.
$\begin{array}{r} 62 \\ \times\ 9 \\ \hline 558 \end{array}$

5.
$\begin{array}{r} 25 \\ \times\ 3 \\ \hline 75 \end{array}$

6.
$\begin{array}{r} 44 \\ \times\ 6 \\ \hline 264 \end{array}$

7.
$\begin{array}{r} 32 \\ \times\ 5 \\ \hline 160 \end{array}$

8.
$\begin{array}{r} 51 \\ \times\ 4 \\ \hline 204 \end{array}$

9.
$\begin{array}{r} 82 \\ \times\ 3 \\ \hline 246 \end{array}$

10.
$\begin{array}{r} 55 \\ \times\ 2 \\ \hline 110 \end{array}$

11.
$\begin{array}{r} 38 \\ \times\ 8 \\ \hline 304 \end{array}$

12.
$\begin{array}{r} 87 \\ \times\ 4 \\ \hline 348 \end{array}$

13. Lea's Bake Shop sells muffins. The shop sells 37 muffins each week for 6 weeks. How many muffins does it sell in all?

222 muffins

Name _____

Learn the Math

You can multiply using place value and partial products.

Example 1 Use place value with regrouping.

Multiply. 5×23 Estimate. $5 \times 20 = 100$

	Model	Think	Record
Step 1		Multiply the ones. 5×3 ones = _____ ones	**1** 23 Regroup the $\times\ \underline{\ 5}$ 15 ones as $\mathbf{5}$ 1 ten 5 ones.
Step 2		Multiply the tens. 5×2 tens = _____ tens Add the regrouped ten. 10 tens + 1 ten = 11 tens	1 23 Regroup 11 tens $\times\ \underline{\ 5}$ as 1 hundred **115** 1 ten.

So, $5 \times 23 = $ _____.

Example 2 Use partial products.

Multiply. 4×23 Estimate. $4 \times 25 = 100$

	Model	Think	Record
Step 1	20 3 / 4	Multiply the tens. 4×2 tens = _____ tens	$\begin{array}{r} 2\,0 \\ \times\ \ 4 \\ \hline \square \end{array}$
Step 2	20 3 / 4	Multiply the ones. 4×3 ones = _____ ones	$\begin{array}{r} 3 \\ \times\ 4 \\ \hline \square \end{array}$
Step 3	20 3 / 4 80 12	Add the partial products.	$\begin{array}{r} 2\,3 \\ \times\ \ 4 \\ \hline 8\,0 \\ +\ 1\,2 \\ \hline \square \end{array}$

So, $4 \times 23 = $ _____.

REASONING Explain how to find 2×42 using partial products.

1. Mr. Spencer ordered 3 boxes of magnets. Each box has 18 magnets in it. How many magnets does he have in all?

Multiply. 3 × 18   Estimate. 3 × 20 = 60

- Multiply the ones.

  3 × 8 ones = _____ ones

  Regroup the ones.

- Multiply the tens.

  3 × 1 ten = _____ tens

  Add the regrouped tens.

  _____ tens + 2 tens = _____ tens

So, Mr. Spencer has _____ magnets in all.

$$
\begin{array}{r}
\square \\
1\,8 \\
\times\ \ 3 \\
\hline
\square\ \square
\end{array}
$$

Find the product.

2.
$$
\begin{array}{r}
2\,3 \\
\times\ \ 7 \\
\hline
\square \\
\square \\
+\ \square \\
\hline
\square
\end{array}
$$

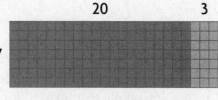

3.
$$
\begin{array}{r}
\square \\
2\,6 \\
\times\ \ 3 \\
\hline
\square
\end{array}
$$

4.
$$
\begin{array}{r}
62 \\
\times\ 9 \\
\hline
\end{array}
$$

5.
$$
\begin{array}{r}
25 \\
\times\ 3 \\
\hline
\end{array}
$$

6.
$$
\begin{array}{r}
44 \\
\times\ 6 \\
\hline
\end{array}
$$

7.
$$
\begin{array}{r}
32 \\
\times\ 5 \\
\hline
\end{array}
$$

8.
$$
\begin{array}{r}
51 \\
\times\ 4 \\
\hline
\end{array}
$$

9.
$$
\begin{array}{r}
82 \\
\times\ 3 \\
\hline
\end{array}
$$

10.
$$
\begin{array}{r}
55 \\
\times\ 2 \\
\hline
\end{array}
$$

11.
$$
\begin{array}{r}
38 \\
\times\ 8 \\
\hline
\end{array}
$$

12.
$$
\begin{array}{r}
87 \\
\times\ 4 \\
\hline
\end{array}
$$

13. Lea's Bake Shop sells muffins. The shop sells 37 muffins each week for 6 weeks. How many muffins does it sell in all?

_____

Objective
To read and write fractions

Vocabulary
denominator The part of the fraction below the line that tells how many equal parts there are in the whole or in the group

numerator The part of the fraction above the line that tells how many parts are being counted

COMMON ERROR

- Students may write the numerator correctly but may write the denominator as the unshaded parts of the model.

- To correct this, have students write the denominator first, emphasizing that it is the total number of equal parts.

Learn the Math page IN111 Remind students that a fraction can name parts of a whole or parts of a group. Review the terms *numerator* and *denominator*. Ask: **How do you know what number to record in the denominator of the fraction?** The denominator is the number of equal parts in the whole or in the group. **How do you know what number to record in the numerator of the fraction?** The numerator is the number of equal parts being counted. Guide students through the example. Ask: **Into how many equal parts is the coffee cake divided?** 10 **How many of the equal parts are not eaten?** 3 **What fraction can you**

write to represent the amount of coffee cake left? $\frac{3}{10}$ Emphasize that a fraction can be read in different ways. Discuss that fractions can name parts of a whole or parts of a group.

REASONING Invite volunteers to share their explanations with the class. Ask: **How can you find the fraction of the pizza that was eaten?** Possible answer: there were 8 slices of pizza and 1 slice is left. I can subtract $8 - 1 = 7$ to find the number of slices eaten. So, $\frac{7}{8}$ of the pizza was eaten.

Do the Math page IN112 Guide students through Exercise 1. Point out that this problem involves finding part of a group and the coffee-cake problem involves finding parts of a whole.

Assign Exercises 2–13 and monitor students' work.

Discuss Problem 14 with the students. Ask: **How many stickers are there in all?** 8 **How many of the stickers are hearts?** 3 **What fraction can you write?** $\frac{3}{8}$

Students who make more than 4 errors in Exercises 1–14 may benefit from the **Alternative Teaching Strategy**.

Alternative Teaching Strategy
Manipulatives: two-color counters, fraction circles

Have each student place counters so that 2 are one color and 3 are the other color. Ask students to describe the parts of the group by using words and phrases such as the following: 2 out of 5 are red; 3 out 5 are yellow; 2 divided by 5; 3 divided by 5; $\frac{2}{5}$; $\frac{3}{5}$. Repeat, using different numbers of counters. Then use fraction circles to represent parts of a whole.

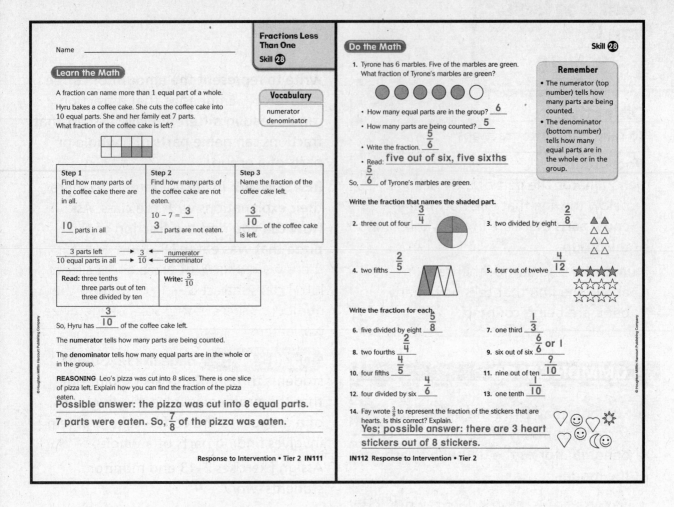

Learn the Math

A fraction can name more than 1 equal part of a whole.

Hyru bakes a coffee cake. She cuts the coffee cake into 10 equal parts. She and her family eat 7 parts.
What fraction of the coffee cake is left?

Vocabulary

numerator
denominator

Step 1	Step 2	Step 3
Find how many parts of the coffee cake there are in all.	Find how many parts of the coffee cake are not eaten.	Name the fraction of the coffee cake left.
__10__ parts in all	$10 - 7 = \dfrac{3}{3}$ parts are not eaten.	$\dfrac{3}{10}$ of the coffee cake is left.

3 parts left $\longrightarrow$ 3 $\longleftarrow$ numerator
10 equal parts in all $\longrightarrow$ 10 $\longleftarrow$ denominator

Read: three tenths three parts out of ten three divided by ten	**Write:** $\dfrac{3}{10}$

So, Hyru has $\dfrac{3}{10}$ of the coffee cake left.

The **numerator** tells how many parts are being counted.

The **denominator** tells how many equal parts are in the whole or in the group.

REASONING Leo's pizza was cut into 8 slices. There is one slice of pizza left. Explain how you can find the fraction of the pizza eaten.

Possible answer: the pizza was cut into 8 equal parts.
7 parts were eaten. So, $\dfrac{7}{8}$ of the pizza was eaten.

Do the Math

Skill 28

1. Tyrone has 6 marbles. Five of the marbles are green. What fraction of Tyrone's marbles are green?

- How many equal parts are in the group? __6__
- How many parts are being counted? __5__
- Write the fraction. $\dfrac{5}{6}$
- Read: **five out of six, five sixths**

So, $\dfrac{5}{6}$ of Tyrone's marbles are green.

Remember
- The numerator (top number) tells how many parts are being counted.
- The denominator (bottom number) tells how many equal parts are in the whole or in the group.

Write the fraction that names the shaded part.

2. three out of four $\dfrac{3}{4}$

3. two divided by eight $\dfrac{2}{8}$

4. two fifths $\dfrac{2}{5}$

5. four out of twelve $\dfrac{4}{12}$

Write the fraction for each.

6. five divided by eight $\dfrac{5}{8}$

7. one third $\dfrac{1}{3}$

8. two fourths $\dfrac{2}{4}$

9. six out of six $\dfrac{6}{6}$ or 1

10. four fifths $\dfrac{4}{5}$

11. nine out of ten $\dfrac{9}{10}$

12. four divided by six $\dfrac{4}{6}$

13. one tenth $\dfrac{1}{10}$

14. Fay wrote $\dfrac{3}{8}$ to represent the fraction of the stickers that are hearts. Is this correct? Explain.
Yes; possible answer: there are 3 heart
stickers out of 8 stickers.

Equivalent Fractions
Skill 29

Objective
To model and write fractions

Vocabulary
equivalent fractions Two or more
fractions that name the same amount

Manipulatives
fraction strips

COMMON ERROR

- Students may incorrectly line up the
  fraction strips.

- To correct this, be sure students align
  the first fraction strip flush left with
  the strip for 1 whole. Remind them
  to check the alignment again after
  placing each new fraction strip.

Learn the Math page IN115 Read
the introductory text and problem with
students. Show students how to use
fraction strips to determine equivalent
fractions. Ask: **How many $\frac{1}{10}$ strips can you
place under the two $\frac{1}{5}$ strips so they
line up end to end?** four $\frac{1}{10}$ strips Guide
students to use the fraction strips to show
other examples of equivalent fractions.

REASONING Discuss the question with
students. Ask: **What do you notice about
the numerators and the denominators?**
Possible answer: both the numerator
and the denominator double from one
fraction to the next. Encourage students
to model each of the fractions with
fraction strips to show that they are
equivalent.

Do the Math page IN116 Read and
discuss Exercise 1 with students. Guide
students in solving the problem. Ask: **How
do you know what fraction to write?**
Possible answer: the numerator is the
number of $\frac{1}{6}$ strips I used. Since I used
$\frac{1}{6}$ strips, the denominator is 6. **What other
fraction strips could you use to show $\frac{1}{3}$?**
Possible answer: twelfths

Assign Exercises 2–7 and monitor students'
work.

Discuss Problems 8 and 9 with the
students. Have students use fraction strips
to model each. In Problem 9, ask students
to think about whether they need to use
a fraction strip that represents a smaller
or a larger fraction. After students have
found the answer, ask: **How do you
know that Manu used six $\frac{1}{12}$ strips?**
Possible answer: when I line up the
strips, six $\frac{1}{12}$ strips name the same amount
as one $\frac{1}{2}$ strip.

Students who make more than 2 errors
in Exercises 1–9 may benefit from the
Alternative Teaching Strategy.

Alternative Teaching Strategy
Manipulatives: fraction circles

Have students use fraction circles to find
equivalent fractions. Ask students to
identify the $\frac{1}{2}$ circle. Ask: **What fractions
are equivalent to $\frac{1}{2}$?** Have students
place fraction pieces of the same type
on top of the $\frac{1}{2}$ circle to find equivalent
fractions. When they find an equivalent
fraction, have them trace the fraction
pieces on paper and write the fraction
below the model. Encourage students to
find as many equivalent fractions as they
can for $\frac{1}{2}$. Repeat for other equivalent
fractions.

Name _____

Learn the Math

Two or more fractions that name the same amount are called **equivalent fractions**.

Jack made a loaf of sourdough bread. For dinner, his family ate $\frac{2}{5}$ of the bread. Find a fraction that is equivalent to $\frac{2}{5}$.

You can use fraction strips to find equivalent fractions.

Vocabulary

equivalent fractions

Step 1	Step 2
Start with the strip for 1 whole. Line up two $\frac{1}{5}$ strips to show $\frac{2}{5}$.	Try $\frac{1}{10}$ strips. Line up $\frac{1}{10}$ strips to show the same amount as $\frac{2}{5}$.

Step 3

Count the number of $\frac{1}{10}$ strips that show the same amount as $\frac{2}{5}$.

Count: $\frac{1}{10}, \frac{2}{10}, \frac{3}{10}, \frac{4}{10}$

Write the equivalent fraction.

Write: $\frac{2}{5} = \frac{4}{10}$

So, $\frac{4}{10}$ is equivalent to $\frac{2}{5}$.

REASONING What pattern do you see in the following fractions? $\frac{1}{3}, \frac{2}{6}, \frac{4}{12}$

Possible answer: both the numerator and the denominator double from one fraction to the next. They are all equivalent fractions.

Do the Math

1. Addie ate $\frac{1}{3}$ of her sandwich for lunch. Find a fraction that is equivalent to $\frac{1}{3}$.

- Use fraction strips to show 1 whole. Then use fraction strips to show $\frac{1}{3}$.

- Can you use $\frac{1}{6}$ fraction strips to show $\frac{1}{3}$? __yes__

- How many $\frac{1}{6}$ strips do you need to show $\frac{1}{3}$? __2__

- What is the equivalent fraction? __$\frac{2}{6}$__

So, $\frac{2}{6}$ is equivalent to $\frac{1}{3}$.

Remember

- Line up the fraction strips at the left.
- The number of fraction strips represents the numerator of the equivalent fraction.

Write two equivalent fractions for each picture. **Possible answers are given.**

2. $\frac{3}{4}, \frac{6}{8}$

3. $\frac{8}{10}, \frac{12}{15}$

4. $\frac{2}{3}, \frac{8}{12}$

5. $\frac{3}{4}, \frac{12}{12}$

6. $\frac{1}{3}, \frac{2}{6}$

7. $\frac{1}{2}, \frac{2}{4}$

8. Marta measures an ant that is $\frac{1}{4}$ inch long. How many eighths of an inch long is the ant?

$\frac{2}{8}$ inch

9. Manu used 6 of the same type of fraction strip to show $\frac{1}{2}$. What type of fraction strip did he use?

a $\frac{1}{12}$ fraction strip

Draw a Diagram • Multiply 2-Digit Numbers

Problem Solving Strategy 1

Objective

To use the strategy *draw a diagram* to solve multiplication problems

Materials

grid paper (see *Teacher Resources*)

COMMON ERROR

- Some students may have difficulty translating from a problem situation in words to a diagram.

- To correct this, have students count rows to represent each section on different parts of the grid paper. Have them cut out the models and then overlay the smaller section on the larger grid and shade it.

Problem Solving   page IN118

Read the Problem

• **What do I need to find?** Read and discuss the problem with the students. Ask: **What question do you need to answer?** How many seats are not reserved?

• **What information do I need to use?** Have students identify the information they need to solve the problem. Say: **Describe the number of rows and the number of seats in each row for each section.** entire section: 9 rows of 16 seats; reserved section: 3 rows of 6 seats

• **How will I use the information?** Have students make a plan to use the information given to solve the problem.

Ask: **How can you find the number of seats that are not reserved?** Possible answer: I can draw a diagram of the two sections and multiply to find the number of seats in each section. Then I can subtract to find the difference.

Solve the Problem

Have students draw a diagram to show the number of seats in each section and shade the reserved section. Ask: **How can you find the number of seats not reserved?** Possible answer: multiply to find the total number of seats in the larger section and the number of seats in the reserved section. Then subtract the two products to find how many seats are not reserved. **How can the strategy *draw a diagram* help you solve multiplication problems?** Possible answer: the diagram helps you visualize the area model used in multiplication and helps you recognize the additional step needed in a multi-step problem.

Assign Exercises 1–2 and monitor students' work. Students who make more than 1 error in Exercises 1–2 may benefit from the **Alternative Teaching Strategy**.

Alternative Teaching Strategy

Materials: scissors, grid paper (see *Teacher Resources*)

Have students draw the diagram on grid paper, cut out the entire diagram, and then cut out the reserved section separately. Show them how to overlay the reserved section. Explain that the remaining part of the diagram is the section not reserved. Relate removing the reserved section to subtracting those seats from the whole. Practice with similar problems.

For answer page, see page IN123.

Name _____

Problem Solving

There are 9 rows of 16 seats in a section of the school auditorium. Six seats in the center of the first 3 rows are reserved. How many seats are not reserved?

Read the Problem	Solve the Problem
What do I need to find? I need to find the _____ _____.	I drew a diagram to show 9 rows of 16 seats. I shaded a section to show the 3 rows of 6 seats that are reserved.
What information do I need to use? There are _____ rows of _____ seats in a section of the school auditorium. There are _____ rows with _____ seats in each row in the reserved section.	I found the total number of seats in the section and the number of seats in the reserved section. $9 \times 16 =$ _____ $3 \times 6 =$ _____ What else do you need to do to solve the problem?
How will I use the information? I can _____ to find both the number of seats in the section of the auditorium and the number of seats in the reserved section.	_____ So, _____ seats are not reserved.

Draw a diagram to solve.

1. A section of bleachers has 12 rows of 10 seats. Each of the first 3 bleachers has 6 seats reserved for faculty. How many seats in the section are not reserved?

   _____

2. The seats in sections A and B of the auditorium are reserved for student volunteers. Section A has 4 rows of 12 seats. Section B has 5 rows of 8 seats. How many people can sit in Sections A and B?

   _____

Make a Chart • Decimals

Problem Solving Strategy 2

Objective
To use the strategy *make a chart* to solve problems involving decimals

Materials
number lines (see *Teacher Resources*)

COMMON ERROR

- Some students may have difficulty identifying all possible tenths digits.

- To correct this, have students use a number line divided into tenths. Students can label the two numbers given and shade between the two points to help identify the tenths digits.

Problem Solving   page IN120

Read the Problem
- **What do I need to find?** Read and discuss the problem with students.
Ask: **What question do you need to answer?** What number matches the clues?

- **What information do I need to use?** Have students identify the information they need to solve the problem.
Ask: **What are the clues?** The number is between 2.3 and 2.6. It has three digits. The product of the tenths digit and the hundredths digit is 35.

- **How will I use the information?** Have students make a plan for solving the problem. Ask: **How can you find the number?** Possible answer: I can make a place-value chart to show all possible tenths in the first clue. Then I can use the second clue to test each tenth until I find the correct hundredth.

Solve the Problem
Have students make a place-value chart and fill in the ones digit and the possible tenths digits. Ask: **How can you find the hundredths digit?** Possible answer: I can test each tenths digit to find a 1-digit whole number that makes the equation "tenths digit $\times$ hundredths digit = 35" true. **How can the strategy *make a chart* help you solve problems like these?** Possible answer: the chart helps you see all possible numbers so you can make sure you test each one.

Assign Exercises 1–2 and monitor students' work. Students who make more than 1 error in Exercises 1–2 may benefit from the **Alternative Teaching Strategy**.

Alternative Teaching Strategy
Manipulatives and Materials: counters, number lines (see *Teacher Resources*)

Have students use a number line to find all possible tenths digits. Then have them use counters to model each possible equation.

For answer page, see page IN123.

Name _____

Problem Solving

Ricardo's sister asked him this number riddle. What is the number?

Clues
- A number is between 2.3 and 2.6 and has three digits.
- The product of the digit in the tenths place and the digit in the hundredths place is 35.

Read the Problem		
What do I need to find? I need to find a _____ that matches the clues.	**What information do I need to use?** Underline the information listed in the *Clues* that you will use.	**How will I use the information?** I can _____ and use the clues to help me find the number.

Solve the Problem

I made a chart to show the possible tenths digits: 3, 4, 5.

Ones	.	Tenths	Hundredths
2	.	3	
2	.	4	
2	.	5	

Think: 3 × ___ = 35   Is there a 1-digit whole number that makes the equation true? _____

Think: 4 × ___ = 35   Is there a 1-digit whole number that makes the equation true? _____

Think: 5 × ___ = 35   Is there a 1-digit whole number that makes the equation true? _____

The number _____ is between 2.3 and 2.6. The product of _____ ,

the digit in the tenths place, and _____ , the digit in the hundredths

place, is 35. So, the number is _____ .

Make a chart to solve.

1. A three-digit number is between 8.7 and 9. The product of the tenths digit and the hundredths digit is 9. What is the number?

2. A four-digit number is between 24.1 and 24.4. The sum of the tenths digit and the hundredths digit is 12. What is the number?

_____

_____

Make a Table • Relate Perimeter and Area

Problem Solving Strategy 3

Objective

To use the strategy *make a table* to solve problems that relate perimeter and area

COMMON ERROR

- Students may assume that all rectangles with the same perimeter will also have the same area.

- To correct this, have students analyze drawings of rectangles that have different lengths and widths, but the same perimeter. Have them find the area of each rectangle to show that the areas of the shapes vary.

Problem Solving   page IN122

Read the Problem

• **What do I need to find?** Read and discuss the problem with the students. Ask: **What question do you need to answer?** What is the length and the width of a rectangle that has the greatest area when the perimeter is 32 feet?

• **What information do I need to use?** Have students identify the information they need to solve the problem. **What is the perimeter of the reading zone?** 32 feet

• **How will I use the information?** Have students make a plan to use the information given to solve the problem. Ask: **How can you find the greatest area?** Possible answer: I can make a table to show the length and width of some rectangles that have a perimeter of 32 feet. Then I can find the area of each rectangle and choose the one that has the greatest area.

Solve the Problem

Have students complete the table with length, width, perimeter, and area. Ask: **What pattern do you notice in the table as the length decreases and the width increases?** Possible answer: I found that as the length and the width become closer in measure, the area increases. **How can the strategy *make a table* help you solve problems?** Possible answer: it helps you organize the information in a problem and allows you to see patterns that help solve the problem.

Assign Exercises 1–2 and monitor students' work.

Students who make more than 1 error in Exercises 1–2 may benefit from the **Alternative Teaching Strategy**.

Alternative Teaching Strategy

Manipulatives: grid paper (see *Teacher Resources*)

Have students work in pairs to draw all possible rectangles with sides that are whole numbers and have a perimeter of 32 units on grid paper. Direct them to label the length and the width and calculate the area of each rectangle. They should write the area in square units and record it in the center of each rectangle. Then ask the students which rectangle has the greatest area. Repeat the activity with rectangles that have perimeters of 12 units and 8 units.

For answer page, see page IN123.

Name _____

Problem Solving

Mrs. Cason is creating a rectangular reading zone in the school library. What is the greatest area the reading zone can have if the perimeter, or the distance around the zone, is exactly 32 feet? Find its length and width in whole numbers.

Read the Problem	Solve the Problem
What do I need to find? I need to find the length and width of the reading zone with the greatest _____ when the perimeter is 32 feet.	I made a table to show the lengths and widths of rectangles that have a perimeter of 32 feet.

What information do I need to use?

The perimeter of the reading zone is exactly _____.

How will I use the information?

I can _____ to search for a pattern.

Perimeter and Area				
Zone	Length (in ft)	Width (in ft)	Perimeter (in ft)	Area (in sq ft)
A	15	1	32	15
B	14	2	____	28
C	____	3	32	____
D	12	__	32	____
E	11	5	32	____
F	10	6	32	____
G	9	__	32	____
H	__	8	32	____

From the table, I can see that as the length and the width become closer in measure, the area _____.

So, the greatest area for the reading zone is _____ square feet. It has a length of _____ and a width of _____.

Make a table to solve.

1. Dante wants to place a border around the flowers in his yard. The area he wants bordered is 24 square feet. What is the least amount of border needed? Find its length and width in whole numbers.

   _____

2. Brian is creating a sandbox for his little brother. He has 28 feet of brick to border the sandbox. What is the greatest area that he can make for the sandbox? Find its length and width in whole numbers.

   _____

Panel 1

Name _____

Problem Solving

There are 9 rows of 16 seats in a section of the school auditorium. Six seats in the center of the first 3 rows are reserved. How many seats are not reserved?

Read the Problem	Solve the Problem
What do I need to find? I need to find the **number of seats not reserved**	I drew a diagram to show 9 rows of 16 seats. I shaded a section to show the 3 rows of 6 seats that are reserved. I found the total number of seats in the section and the number of seats in the reserved section. $9 \times 16 =$ **144** $3 \times 6 =$ **18** What else do you need to do to solve the problem? **Subtract. 144 − 18 = 126** So, **126** seats are not reserved.
What information do I need to use? There are **9** rows of **16** seats in a section of the school auditorium. There are **3** rows with **6** seats in each row in the reserved section.	
How will I use the information? I can **multiply** to find both the number of seats in the section of the auditorium and the number of seats in the reserved section.	

Draw a diagram to solve.

1. A section of bleachers has 12 rows of 10 seats. Each of the first 3 bleachers has 6 seats reserved for faculty. How many seats in the section are not reserved?

   102 seats

2. The seats in sections A and B of the auditorium are reserved for student volunteers. Section A has 4 rows of 12 seats. Section B has 5 rows of 8 seats. How many people can sit in Sections A and B?

   88 people

Panel 2

Name _____

Problem Solving

Ricardo's sister asked him this number riddle. What is the number?

Clues
- A number is between 2.3 and 2.6 and has three digits.
- The product of the digit in the tenths place and the digit in the hundredths place is 35.

Read the Problem		
What do I need to find? I need to find a **number** that matches the clues.	**What information do I need to use?** Underline the information listed in the *Clues* that you will use.	**How will I use the information?** I can **make a chart** and use the clues to help me find the number.

Solve the Problem

I made a chart to show the possible tenths digits: 3, 4, 5.

Ones	.	Tenths	Hundredths
2	.	3	
2	.	4	
2	.	5	

Think: $3 \times \_\_ = 35$ Is there a 1-digit whole number that makes the equation true? **no**
Think: $4 \times \_\_ = 35$ Is there a 1-digit whole number that makes the equation true? **no**
Think: $5 \times$ **7** $= 35$ Is there a 1-digit whole number that makes the equation true? **yes**

The number **2.57** is between 2.3 and 2.6 and the product of **5**, the digit in the tenths place, and **7**, the digit in the hundredths place, is 35. So, the number is **2.57**.

Make a chart to solve.

1. A three-digit number is between 8.7 and 9. The product of the tenths digit and the hundredths digit is 9. What is the number?

   8.91

2. A four-digit number is between 24.1 and 24.4. The sum of the tenths digit and the hundredths digit is 12. What is the number?

   24.39

Panel 3

Name _____

Problem Solving

Mrs. Cason is creating a rectangular reading zone in the school library. What is the greatest area the reading zone can have if the perimeter, or the distance around the zone, is exactly 32 feet? Find its length and width in whole numbers.

Read the Problem	Solve the Problem
What do I need to find? I need to find the length and width of the reading zone with the greatest **area** when the perimeter is 32 feet.	I made a table to show the lengths and widths of rectangles that have a perimeter of 32 feet.
What information do I need to use? The perimeter of the reading zone is exactly **32 feet**.	
How will I use the information? I can **make a table** to search for a pattern.	

Perimeter and Area			
Zone	Length (in ft)	Width (in ft)	Perimeter (in ft)	Area (in sq ft)
A	15	1	32	15
B	14	2	**32**	28
C	**13**	3	32	**39**
D	12	**4**	32	**48**
E	11	5	32	**55**
F	10	6	32	**60**
G	9	**7**	32	**63**
H	**8**	8	32	**64**

From the table, I can see that as the length and the width become closer in measure, the area **increases**.

So, the greatest area for the reading zone is **64** square feet. It has a length of **8 feet** and a width of **8 feet**.

Make a table to solve.

1. Dante wants to place a border around the flowers in his yard. The area he wants bordered is 24 square feet. What is the least amount of border needed? Find its length and width in whole numbers.

   20 feet; 6 ft × 4 ft

2. Brian is creating a sandbox for his little brother. He has 28 feet of brick to border the sandbox. What is the greatest area that he can make for the sandbox? Find its length and width in whole numbers.

   49 square feet; 7 ft × 7 ft

Objective
To regroup hundreds as tens

Manipulatives
base-ten blocks

COMMON ERROR

- Students may count the tens incorrectly after regrouping.

- To correct this, have students use base-ten blocks to model the numbers. Then have them skip count by tens to count each hundreds block. When they reach the ten rods, have them count these individually. For example, for 4 hundreds 6 tens, count 10, 20, 30, 40, 41, 42, 43, 44, 45, 46 tens.

Learn the Math page IN127 Read the problem with students. Provide them with base-ten blocks. Ask: **How can you use the model to complete the place-value chart?** Count the number of hundreds blocks for the hundreds and the number of tens rods for the tens. Have students regroup 2 hundreds as tens. Ask: **How many tens are in 2 hundreds?** 20 tens Ask: **How many tens are in 2 hundreds 5 tens?** 25 tens Have students write the tens in the place-value chart. They can refer to the chart to complete the final answer.

REASONING Elicit that Carlos did not regroup all of the hundreds as tens. Ask: **How can you decide if Carlos is correct?** Possible answer: model the number with base-ten blocks. Regroup 2 hundreds as

20 tens. Then count the number of hundreds and tens in the model.

Do the Math page IN128 Read and discuss Exercise 1 with students. Ask: **What are you asked to find?** the number of pages Felicia has in her scrapbook Elicit that students must find how many tens are in 340 to solve. Ask: **How do you know that 3 hundreds 4 tens is the same as 34 tens?** Possible answer: when I regroup 3 hundreds as 30 tens, there are 34 tens in all.

Assign Exercises 2–9 and monitor students' work.

Discuss Problem 10 with students. Explain that they must find the number of tens in 1 hundred 8 tens to solve. Ask: **How many days does it take Taylor to read the book?** 18 days Encourage students to explain their solution methods.

Students who make more than 2 errors in Exercises 1–10 may benefit from the **Alternative Teaching Strategy**.

Alternative Teaching Strategy
Manipulatives and Materials: base-ten blocks, place-value charts (see *Teacher Resources*)

Have students work in pairs. Give each pair several hundreds blocks and tens rods. Ask students to write the number of hundreds and tens in a place-value chart. Then have students regroup each hundreds block as 10 tens rods. Students should then count the total number of tens rods and record the number in a place-value chart. Discuss how the charts are similar and how they are different.

Name _____

Learn the Math

You can use models and a place-value chart to regroup hundreds as tens.

Regroup 250 as tens.

- The model shows 250. Use the model to write the number of hundreds and tens in the place-value chart.

Hundreds	Tens	Ones
2	5	0

- Regroup each hundred as 10 tens.

- Write the number of tens in the place-value chart.

Hundreds	Tens	Ones
	25	0

So, __2__ hundreds __5__ tens = __25__ tens.

REASONING Carlos says that 4 hundreds 3 tens is the same as 2 hundreds 23 tens. Is he correct? Explain.

Yes; possible answer: if you regroup 2 of the hundreds as 20 tens, there will be 2 hundreds 23 tens.

Skill 30

1. Felicia has 340 pictures to put in her scrapbook. She puts 10 pictures on each page. How many pages of pictures does she have in her scrapbook?

Remember
Regroup 1 hundred as 10 tens.

- Complete the place-value chart.
  How many hundreds and tens are in 340?
  __3__ hundreds __4__ tens

Hundreds	Tens	Ones
3	4	0

- Regroup. How many tens are in 3 hundreds?
  __30__

- Complete the place-value chart.
  How many tens are in 3 hundreds 4 tens?
  __34__ tens

Hundreds	Tens	Ones
	34	0

So, Felicia has __34__ pages of pictures.

Regroup. Write the missing numbers.

2. 4 hundreds 6 tens = __46__ tens
3. 1 hundred 8 tens = __18__ tens

4. 5 hundreds 2 tens = __52__ tens
5. 2 hundreds 9 tens = __29__ tens

6. 7 hundreds 1 ten = __71__ tens
7. 6 hundreds 3 tens = __63__ tens

8. 4 hundreds 7 tens = __47__ tens
9. 5 hundreds 6 tens = __56__ tens

10. Taylor is reading a book with 180 pages. He reads 10 pages each day. How many days does it take Taylor to read the whole book?

__18__ days

Name _____

Learn the Math

You can use models and a place-value chart to regroup hundreds as tens.

Regroup 250 as tens.

- The model shows 250. Use the model to write the number of hundreds and tens in the place-value chart.

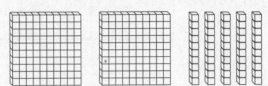

Hundreds	Tens	Ones
		0

- Regroup each hundred as 10 tens.

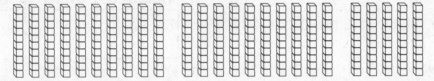

- Write the number of tens in the place-value chart.

Hundreds	Tens	Ones
		0

So, _____ hundreds _____ tens = _____ tens.

REASONING Carlos says that 4 hundreds 3 tens is the same as 2 hundreds 23 tens. Is he correct? Explain.

_____

_____

1. Felicia has 340 pictures to put in her scrapbook. She puts 10 pictures on each page. How many pages of pictures does she have in her scrapbook?

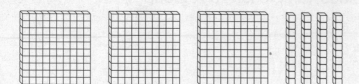

- Complete the place-value chart.

  How many hundreds and tens are in 340?

  _____ hundreds _____ tens

Hundreds	Tens	Ones
		0

- Regroup. How many tens are in 3 hundreds?

  _____ tens

- Complete the place-value chart.

  How many tens are in 3 hundreds 4 tens?

  _____ tens

Hundreds	Tens	Ones
		0

So, Felicia has _____ pages of pictures.

Regroup. Write the missing numbers.

2. 4 hundreds 6 tens = _____ tens   3. 1 hundred 8 tens = _____ tens

4. 5 hundreds 2 tens = _____ tens   5. 2 hundreds 9 tens = _____ tens

6. 7 hundreds 1 ten = _____ tens   7. 6 hundreds 3 tens = _____ tens

8. 4 hundreds 7 tens = _____ tens   9. 5 hundreds 6 tens = _____ tens

10. Taylor is reading a book with 180 pages. He reads 10 pages each day. How many days does it take Taylor to read the whole book?

_____ days

Objective
To add and subtract 2-digit numbers

COMMON ERRORS

- Students may use the wrong operation to solve a story problem.

- To correct this, remind students that they should use addition to find a total, and subtraction to compare two numbers.

- Students may write the 2-digit sum in the ones column, rather than regrouping at the top of the tens column.

- To correct this, remind students to regroup the ones as tens and to put the regrouped tens digit over the tens column. Students may better understand this concept if they use base-ten blocks to model the problem.

Learn the Math page IN131 Read and discuss both questions. Ask: **What do you need to find out in the first question?** how many tickets Pablo and Tasha sell in all **Do you add or subtract to find a total?** add Guide the students through each of the steps to add the two numbers.

Then ask: **What do you need to find out in the second question?** how many more tickets Pablo sells than Tasha **What operation do you need to use to solve this question?** I am comparing two numbers, so I need to use subtraction. Guide the students through each of the steps to subtract the two numbers.

REASONING Remind students that when they need to regroup to subtract, they must write the regrouping correctly.

Do the Math page IN132 Read and discuss Exercise 1 with students. Ask: **What are you asked to do?** Add for the first question and then subtract. Guide students to answer the questions.

Assign Exercises 2–13 and monitor students' work.

Discuss Problem 14 with students. Remind them that when you estimate a sum of 2-digit numbers, you round each addend to the nearest ten. If students are having difficulty, use a number line to round.

Students who make more than 4 errors in Exercises 1–14 may benefit from the **Alternative Teaching Strategy**.

Alternative Teaching Strategy
Manipulatives: base-ten blocks

Have students work in pairs to use base-ten blocks to solve $32 - 18$ written in vertical form. Have partners model 3 tens 2 ones. Ask: **Which column do you subtract first?** the ones **Do you have enough ones to subtract 8 from 2?** no

Have partners trade 1 tens rod for 10 unit cubes to show regrouping 1 ten as 10 ones. Then have partners remove 8 unit cubes to show $12 - 8 = 4$. Ask: **How many ones do you have left?** 4

Have students record the number 4 under the ones column.

Then ask: **How many tens do you subtract?** 1 **How many tens do you have left?** 1 Have students record the number 1 under the tens column for the problem. Ask: **What do you have left?** 1 ten 4 ones, or 14

Repeat with similar problems including addition problems that involve regrouping.

Learn the Math

Pablo and Tasha are selling tickets for the drama club. Pablo sells 77 tickets. Tasha sells 58 tickets. How many tickets do Pablo and Tasha sell in all? How many more tickets does Pablo sell than Tasha?

How many tickets do Pablo and Tasha sell in all?

Use place value. Add 77 + 58.

Step 1	Step 2
Add the ones.	Add the tens.
7 + 8 = 15 ones	1 + 7 + 5 = 13 tens
$\begin{array}{r}1\\77\\+58\\\hline 5\end{array}$	$\begin{array}{r}11\\77\\+58\\\hline 135\end{array}$
Regroup 15 ones as 1 ten 5 ones.	Regroup 13 tens as 1 hundred 3 tens.

So, Pablo and Tasha sell __135__ tickets in all.

How many more tickets does Pablo sell than Tasha?

Use place value. Subtract 77 − 58.

Step 1	Step 2
Since 8 > 7, regroup 77 as 6 tens and 17 ones.	Subtract the ones. Subtract the tens.
$\begin{array}{r}6\ 17\\\cancel{77}\\-5\ 8\\\hline\end{array}$	$\begin{array}{r}6\ 17\\\cancel{77}\\-5\ 8\\\hline 1\ 9\end{array}$

So, Pablo sells __19__ more tickets than Tasha.

REASONING Roxanne has 32 pencils. Peter has 15 pencils. Roxanne says she has 27 more pencils than Peter. Is she correct? Explain.

No; possible response: 32 − 15 = 17. Roxanne did not change 3 tens to 2 tens when she regrouped.

Do the Math

1. Lacey and Gabe are collecting cans for the school food drive. Lacey collects 25 cans. Gabe collects 75 cans. How many cans do they collect in all? How many more cans does Gabe collect than Lacey?

• How do you find how many cans Lacey and Gabe collect in all? __add 25 + 75__

• How do you find how many more cans Gabe collects than Lacey? __subtract 75 − 25__

• How many cans do Lacey and Gabe collect in all? __100__

• How many more cans does Gabe collect than Lacey? __50__

> **Remember**
> • Be sure to read the question carefully to decide if you need to add or subtract.
> • Remember to regroup if you need to.

Find the sum.

2. $\begin{array}{r}1\\42\\+39\\\hline 81\end{array}$	3. $\begin{array}{r}34\\+24\\\hline 58\end{array}$	4. $\begin{array}{r}1\\72\\+18\\\hline 90\end{array}$	5. $\begin{array}{r}1\\45\\+27\\\hline 72\end{array}$

Find the difference.

6. $\begin{array}{r}3\ 15\\\cancel{45}\\-27\\\hline 18\end{array}$	7. $\begin{array}{r}4\ 17\\\cancel{57}\\-18\\\hline 39\end{array}$	8. $\begin{array}{r}3\ 12\\\cancel{42}\\-19\\\hline 23\end{array}$	9. $\begin{array}{r}28\\-16\\\hline 12\end{array}$

Problem Solving • Show Your Work

Find the sum or difference.

10. $\begin{array}{r}4\ 13\\\cancel{53}\\-39\\\hline 14\end{array}$	11. $\begin{array}{r}1\\89\\+44\\\hline 133\end{array}$	12. $\begin{array}{r}8\ 13\\\cancel{93}\\-65\\\hline 28\end{array}$	13. $\begin{array}{r}1\\36\\+29\\\hline 65\end{array}$

14. Glenn estimates that the sum of 36 + 21 is 50. Is his estimate reasonable? Why or why not?

No; possible response: if you round each number to the nearest ten, you get 40 + 20 = 60, not 50.

Learn the Math

Pablo and Tasha are selling tickets for the drama club. Pablo sells 77 tickets. Tasha sells 58 tickets. How many tickets do Pablo and Tasha sell in all? How many more tickets does Pablo sell than Tasha?

How many tickets do Pablo and Tasha sell in all?

Use place value. Add 77 + 58.

Step 1	Step 2
Add the ones.	Add the tens.
7 + 8 = 15 ones	1 + 7 + 5 = 13 tens
Regroup 15 ones as 1 ten 5 ones. $\begin{array}{r} \overset{1}{} \\ 77 \\ +\ 58 \\ \hline 5 \end{array}$	Regroup 13 tens as 1 hundred 3 tens. $\begin{array}{r} \overset{1\ 1}{} \\ 77 \\ +\ 58 \\ \hline 135 \end{array}$

So, Pablo and Tasha sell _____ tickets in all.

How many more tickets does Pablo sell than Tasha?

Use place value. Subtract 77 − 58.

Step 1	Step 2
Since 8 > 7, regroup 77 as 6 tens and 17 ones.	Subtract the ones. Subtract the tens.
$\begin{array}{r} \overset{6\ \ 17}{\cancel{77}} \\ -\ 58 \\ \hline \end{array}$	$\begin{array}{r} \overset{6\ \ 17}{\cancel{77}} \\ -\ 58 \\ \hline 1\ 9 \end{array}$

So, Pablo sells _____ more tickets than Tasha.

REASONING Roxanne has 32 pencils. Peter has 15 pencils. Roxanne says she has 27 more pencils than Peter. Is she correct? Explain.

_____

_____

1. Lacey and Gabe are collecting cans for the school food drive. Lacey collects 25 cans. Gabe collects 75 cans. How many cans do they collect in all? How many more cans does Gabe collect than Lacey?

- How do you find how many cans Lacey and Gabe collect in all? _____

- How do you find how many more cans Gabe collects than Lacey? _____

- How many cans do Lacey and Gabe collect in all? _____

- How many more cans does Gabe collect than Lacey? _____

> **Remember**
> - Be sure to read the question carefully to decide if you need to add or subtract.
> - Remember to regroup if you need to.

Find the sum.

2.	42	3.	34	4.	72	5.	45
	+ 39		+ 24		+ 18		+ 27

Find the difference.

6.	45	7.	57	8.	42	9.	28
	− 27		− 18		− 19		− 16

Problem Solving • Show Your Work

Find the sum or difference.

10.	53	11.	89	12.	93	13.	36
	− 39		+ 44		− 65		+ 29

14. Glenn estimates that the sum of 36 + 21 is 50. Is his estimate reasonable? Why or why not?

_____

_____

Objective

To multiply 2-digit numbers by 1-digit numbers

Manipulatives and Materials

base-ten blocks, grid paper

COMMON ERROR

- Students may write a regrouped number above the incorrect place-value position.

- To correct this, have students write multiplication problems on grid paper. The grid lines will help guide students when regrouping.

Learn the Math page IN135 Discuss the problem with students. Explain that many problems can be solved by using different strategies.

Guide students through One Way. Students can use base-ten blocks to model the problem and to help find the product. Remind students that when they regroup, they need to make sure they write the number to be regrouped above the correct place-value position. Have students compare the product to the estimate. Remind them that since 115 is close to 100 the product is reasonable.

Guide students through Another Way. If students have difficulty finding the partial products, have them count the number of shaded squares in each step. Remind students to compare the product to the estimate to check if it is reasonable.

REASONING Discuss the problem with students. Have them write the problem vertically and show their work. Ask: **Why is the first partial product 80 instead of 8?** Possible answer: I am multiplying 2×4 tens, not 2×4 ones.

Do the Math page IN136 Discuss Problem 1 with students. Ask: **What do you need to do to solve this problem?** Find 3×18. Guide students through multiplying the ones and regrouping, then through multiplying the tens and adding the regrouped tens.

Assign Exercises 2–12 and monitor students' work.

Discuss Problem 13. Ask: **What multiplication problem do you write to find the number of muffins the shop sells in all?** 6×37 Invite student volunteers to show how to find the product using both place-value regrouping and partial products.

Students who make more than 4 errors in Exercises 1–13 may benefit from the **Alternative Teaching Strategy**.

Alternative Teaching Strategy

Manipulatives: two-color counters

Have students use the Distributive Property to break apart factors into numbers that are easy to multiply. Write the problem 7×16 on the board. Have students use counters to model 7 rows of 16 counters. Have them break apart the model to make two smaller groups for the factor 16. Have students break the model between the seventh and eighth columns. Ask: **What two facts are shown by the model?** $7 \times 7 = 49$ and $7 \times 9 = 63$ Instruct students to add the two products to find the product of 7×16. $49 + 63 = 112$ Repeat with similar problems.

Learn the Math

You can multiply using place value and partial products.

One Way Use place value with regrouping.
Multiply. 5×23 Estimate. $5 \times 20 = 100$

	Model	Think	Record
Step 1		Multiply the ones. 5×3 ones = **15** ones	**1** 23 Regroup the $\times\ 5$ 15 ones as $\overline{5}$ 1 ten 5 ones.
Step 2		Multiply the tens. 5×2 tens = **10** tens Add the regrouped ten. 10 tens + 1 ten = 11 tens	1 23 Regroup 11 tens $\times\ 5$ as 1 hundred $\overline{115}$ 1 ten.

So, $5 \times 23 =$ **115**

Another Way Use partial products.
Multiply. 4×23 Estimate. $4 \times 25 = 100$

	Model	Think	Record
Step 1	4 20 3	Multiply the tens. 4×2 tens = **8** tens	2 0 $\times\ 4$ $\boxed{8\,0}$
Step 2	4 20 3	Multiply the ones. 4×3 ones = **12** ones	3 $\times\ 4$ $\boxed{1\,2}$
Step 3	4 20 80 12	Add the partial products.	2 3 $\times\ 4$ 8 0 $+\ 1\,2$ $\boxed{9\,2}$

So, $4 \times 23 =$ **92**

REASONING Explain how to find 2×42 using partial products.
Possible answer: Multiply the tens, 2 × 4 tens = 8 tens, or 80. Multiply the ones, 2 × 2 ones = 4 ones. Then add the partial products, 80 + 4 = 84.

Do the Math

1. Mr. Spencer ordered 3 boxes of magnets. Each box has 18 magnets in it. How many magnets does he have in all?

Multiply. 3×18 Estimate. $3 \times 20 = 60$

• Multiply the ones.
3×8 ones = **24** ones
Regroup the ones.   **2**

• Multiply the tens.   1 8
3×1 ten = **3** tens $\times\ \ 3$
$\overline{5\,4}$
Add the regrouped tens.
3 tens + 2 tens = **5** tens

So, Mr. Spencer has **54** magnets in all.

> **Remember**
> • You can find products using place value with regrouping.
> • You can find products using partial products.

Find the product.

2.   2 3
$\times\ \ 7$
$\boxed{140}$
$+\ \boxed{21}$
$\overline{161}$

7   20   3

3.   1
2 6
$\times\ \ 3$
$\boxed{78}$

4.   6 2
$\times\ \ 9$
558

5.   2 5
$\times\ \ 3$
75

6.   4 4
$\times\ \ 6$
264

7.   3 2
$\times\ \ 5$
160

8.   5 1
$\times\ \ 4$
204

9.   8 2
$\times\ \ 3$
246

10.   5 5
$\times\ \ 2$
110

11.   3 8
$\times\ \ 8$
304

12.   8 7
$\times\ \ 4$
348

13. Lea's Bake Shop sells muffins. The shop sells 37 muffins each week for 6 weeks. How many muffins does it sell in all?

222 muffins

Name _____

Learn the Math

You can multiply using place value and partial products.

One Way Use place value with regrouping.
Multiply. 5×23 Estimate. $5 \times 20 = 100$

Model	Think	Record
Step 1	Multiply the ones. 5×3 ones = _____ ones	**1** 23 Regroup the $\times \ 5$ 15 ones as **5** 1 ten 5 ones.
Step 2	Multiply the tens. 5×2 tens = _____ tens Add the regrouped ten. 10 tens + 1 ten = 11 tens	1 23 Regroup 11 tens $\times \ 5$ as 1 hundred **115** 1 ten.

So, $5 \times 23 =$ _____.

Another Way Use partial products.
Multiply. 4×23 Estimate. $4 \times 25 = 100$

Model	Think	Record
Step 1	Multiply the tens. 4×2 tens = _____ tens	2 0 $\times \ \ 4$ ⬚
Step 2	Multiply the ones. 4×3 ones = _____ ones	3 $\times \ 4$ ⬚
Step 3	Add the partial products.	2 3 $\times \ \ 4$ 8 0 + 1 2 ⬚

So, $4 \times 23 =$ _____.

REASONING Explain how to find 2×42 using partial products.

_____

1. Mr. Spencer ordered 3 boxes of magnets. Each box has 18 magnets in it. How many magnets does he have in all?

   Multiply. 3 × 18   Estimate. 3 × 20 = 60

   - Multiply the ones.

     3 × 8 ones = _____ ones

     Regroup the ones.

   - Multiply the tens.

     3 × 1 ten = _____ tens

     Add the regrouped tens.

     _____ tens + 2 tens = _____ tens

   So, Mr. Spencer has _____ magnets in all.

$$\begin{array}{r} 1\ 8 \\ \times\ \ 3 \\ \hline \end{array}$$

> **Remember**
> - You can find products using place value with regrouping.
> - You can find products using partial products.

Find the product.

2.
$$\begin{array}{r} 2\ 3 \\ \times\ 7 \\ \hline \\ + \\ \hline \end{array}$$

20   3

7

3.
$$\begin{array}{r} \\ 2\ 6 \\ \times\ 3 \\ \hline \end{array}$$

4.
$$\begin{array}{r} 62 \\ \times\ 9 \\ \hline \end{array}$$

5.
$$\begin{array}{r} 25 \\ \times\ 3 \\ \hline \end{array}$$

6.
$$\begin{array}{r} 44 \\ \times\ 6 \\ \hline \end{array}$$

7.
$$\begin{array}{r} 32 \\ \times\ 5 \\ \hline \end{array}$$

8.
$$\begin{array}{r} 51 \\ \times\ 4 \\ \hline \end{array}$$

9.
$$\begin{array}{r} 82 \\ \times\ 3 \\ \hline \end{array}$$

10.
$$\begin{array}{r} 55 \\ \times\ 2 \\ \hline \end{array}$$

11.
$$\begin{array}{r} 38 \\ \times\ 8 \\ \hline \end{array}$$

12.
$$\begin{array}{r} 87 \\ \times\ 4 \\ \hline \end{array}$$

13. Lea's Bake Shop sells muffins. The shop sells 37 muffins each week for 6 weeks. How many muffins does it sell in all?

_____

Objective
To use arrays to find products

Vocabulary
array A set of objects arranged in rows and columns

product The answer in a multiplication problem

Manipulatives
square tiles

COMMON ERROR

- Students may reverse the order of the factors when writing a multiplication sentence for an array.

- To correct this, have students draw an array with 5 rows and 4 columns and have them say *5 rows of 4*. Remind them to write the multiplication sentence in this same order.

Learn the Math page IN139 Discuss the first example with students. Guide students through Step 1. Explain that when objects are arranged in equal rows, they form an array. Explain that the number of rows and the number of tiles in each row are the factors they can multiply to find the product. Remind them that they can also count the total number of tiles in the array to find the product.

For Step 2, ask: **How do you write a multiplication sentence for the array?** Possible answer: The first factor is the number of rows and the second factor is the number of tiles in each row. $3 \times 5 = 15$

In the second example, help the students understand that the number of tiles does not change if you turn the array. You can multiply in any order and get the same product.

REASONING Provide examples of multiplication problems for students to model with square tiles. Point out that changing the order of the factors is the same as turning the array 90 degrees.

Do the Math page IN140 Guide students through Exercise 1. Encourage them to make an array using square tiles. Ask: **What multiplication sentence can you write to find the total number of oatmeal cookies?** $5 \times 6 = 30$

Assign Exercises 2–10 and monitor students' work.

Discuss Problem 11. Encourage students to make an array to find the total number of plants. Ask: **How many rows are in the array?** 3 **How many tiles are in each row?** 6 **What multiplication sentence can you write for the array?** $3 \times 6 = 18$

Students who make more than 3 errors in Exercises 1–11 may benefit from the **Alternative Teaching Strategy**.

Alternative Teaching Strategy
Manipulatives and Materials: square tiles, digit cards numbered 1–9 (See Teacher Resource Book)

Give each pair of students square tiles and a set of digit cards. Have each student select a card. Tell pairs to make an array using the numbers on the cards. The first number selected represents the number of rows and second number selected represents the number of tiles in each row. Once they have modeled the array, ask each pair to write the multiplication sentence shown by the array and to find the product. Ask pairs to share their multiplication sentence and array with the class.

Arrays
Skill 33

Learn the Math

Lewis arranges the chairs in the music room into 3 rows of 5 chairs. How many chairs does he use?

Vocabulary

array
product

Step 1	
Make an array with 3 rows of 5 tiles to show the chairs.	

Step 2	
Write a multiplication sentence to find the total number of tiles.	3 rows of 5 = __15__ __3__ × __5__ = __15__

So, Lewis uses __15__ chairs.

If Lewis arranges the chairs into 5 rows of 3 chairs, how many chairs will he use?

Step 1	
You can turn the array to show 5 rows of 3 tiles.	

Step 2	
Write a multiplication sentence to find the total number of tiles.	__5__ rows of __3__ = __15__ __5__ × __3__ = __15__

So, Lewis will use __15__ chairs.

REASONING Explain how using an array can help you find a product.
Possible answer: The number of rows and the number of tiles in each row represent the factors in a multiplication sentence. You can multiply or count the total number of tiles in an array to find a product.

Response to Intervention • Tier 2 **IN139**

Do the Math

Skill 33

1. Alana is baking oatmeal cookies with her mother for the school fair. She has 5 rows of 6 cookies on a cookie sheet. How many oatmeal cookies is Alana baking?

• How many rows of cookies is Alana baking? __5__

• How many cookies are in each row? __6__

• __5__ rows of __6__ = 30

• __5__ × __6__ = 30

So, Alana is baking __30__ oatmeal cookies.

Remember
• You can multiply the number of rows by the number in each row to find a product.
• You can count the total number of tiles in an array to find a product.

Use the array to find the product.

2. __2__ rows of __2__ = __4__
__2__ × __2__ = __4__

3. __3__ rows of __6__ = __18__
__3__ × __6__ = __18__

4. __3__ rows of __3__ = __9__
__3__ × __3__ = __9__

5. __4__ rows of __8__ = __32__
__4__ × __8__ = __32__

6. __1__ row of __7__ = __7__
__1__ × __7__ = __7__

7. __4__ rows of __4__ = __16__
__4__ × __4__ = __16__

8. __1__ row of __6__ = __6__
__1__ × __6__ = __6__

9. __5__ rows of __5__ = __25__
__5__ × __5__ = __25__

10. __2__ rows of __7__ = __14__
__2__ × __7__ = __14__

11. Jenni plants 3 rows of strawberry plants. She puts 6 plants in each row. How many plants does she plant in all?
18 plants

IN140 Response to Intervention • Tier 2

Name _____

Learn the Math

Lewis arranges the chairs in the music room into
3 rows of 5 chairs. How many chairs does he use?

Vocabulary

array
product

Step 1	
Make an array with 3 rows of 5 tiles to show the chairs.	☐☐☐☐☐ ☐☐☐☐☐ ☐☐☐☐☐
Step 2	
Write a multiplication sentence to find the total number of tiles.	3 rows of 5 = _____ _____ × _____ = _____

So, Lewis uses _____ chairs.

If Lewis arranges the chairs into 5 rows of 3 chairs,
how many chairs will he use?

Step 1	
You can turn the array to show 5 rows of 3 tiles.	☐☐☐ ☐☐☐ ☐☐☐ ☐☐☐ ☐☐☐
Step 2	
Write a multiplication sentence to find the total number of tiles.	_____ rows of _____ = _____ _____ × _____ = _____

So, Lewis will use _____ chairs.

REASONING Explain how using an array can help you find a product.

_____

_____

_____

1. Alana is baking oatmeal cookies with her mother for the school fair. She has 5 rows of 6 cookies on a cookie sheet. How many oatmeal cookies is Alana baking?

   - How many rows of cookies is Alana baking? _____

   - How many cookies are in each row? _____

   - _____ rows of _____ = _____

   - _____ × _____ = _____

   So, Alana is baking _____ oatmeal cookies.

Use the array to find the product.

2.

____ rows of ____ = ____
____ × ____ = ____

3.

____ rows of ____ = ____
____ × ____ = ____

4.

____ rows of ____ = ____
____ × ____ = ____

5.

____ rows of ____ = ____
____ × ____ = ____

6.

____ row of ____ = ____
____ × ____ = ____

7.

____ rows of ____ = ____
____ × ____ = ____

8.

____ row of ____ = ____
____ × ____ = ____

9.

____ rows of ____ = ____
____ × ____ = ____

10.

____ rows of ____ = ____
____ × ____ = ____

11. Jenni plants 3 rows of strawberry plants. She puts 6 plants in each row. How many plants does she plant in all?

_____

Compare Parts of a Whole

Skill 34

Objective
To compare unit fractions by using models

Materials
crayons

COMMON ERRORS

- Students may assume that the fraction with the greater denominator is the greater fraction.

- To correct this, review the definition of denominator. Explain that the more equal parts there are in the whole, the smaller each part will be.

Learn the Math page IN143 Discuss parts of a whole. Guide students through Step 1. Ask: **How many equal parts is Gavin's rope divided into?** 4 equal parts **How many of those parts did Gavin use for his art project?** 1 Ask the same questions about Marco's rope. 8 equal parts; 1 Guide students to see that the shaded part of each fraction strip represents the amount of rope that each boy used. Ask: **Which fraction strip shows more shading?** the strip for $\frac{1}{4}$ Point out that this means that $\frac{1}{4}$ is the greater part of the whole.

REASONING Discuss the question with students. Draw two fraction strips on the board, one twice as long as the other. Divide the shorter strip into 4 parts and the longer strip into 8 parts. Shade one part of each strip. Ask: **What fractions do the fraction strips show?** $\frac{1}{4}$ and $\frac{1}{8}$ **Which fraction strip shows more shading?** They both show the same amount of shading. Explain that a smaller fraction of a bigger

whole can be the same size as or larger than a bigger fraction of a smaller whole. This means you cannot compare fractions of different-sized wholes.

Do the Math page IN144 Read and discuss Exercise 1 with students. Guide students to solve the problem. Ask: **How many parts of each fraction strip should be shaded?** 1

Assign Exercises 2–5 and monitor students' work.

Discuss Problem 6 with students. Draw 3 equal-sized circles on the board. Divide one into halves, one into fourths, and one into eighths. Point out that as the number of equal parts increases, the size of each part decreases.

Students who make more than 2 errors in Exercises 1–6 may benefit from the **Alternative Teaching Strategy**.

Alternative Teaching Strategy
Manipulatives: index card, unlined $8\frac{1}{2}" \times 11"$ paper

Give an index card to each student, showing one of the following fractions:

$$\frac{1}{2} \qquad \frac{1}{3} \qquad \frac{1}{4} \qquad \frac{1}{6}$$

$$\frac{1}{8} \qquad \frac{1}{10} \qquad \frac{1}{12}$$

Draw two equal-sized circles on the board. Have two students divide and shade the circles to show their fractions. Ask: **How can you tell which fraction is greater?** It's the fraction that shows more of the circle shaded.

Have two other students each fold and tear a piece of unlined $8\frac{1}{2}" \times 11"$ paper to show their fractions. Ask: **How can you tell which fraction is greater?** It's the fraction that shows the bigger piece of paper.

Repeat the activity with drawings and paper to compare other fractions.

Name _____

Learn the Math

Gavin and Marco each have equal-sized pieces of rope.
Gavin uses $\frac{1}{4}$ of his rope for an art project. Marco uses $\frac{1}{8}$ of his rope for an art project. Who uses more rope?

A fraction can name a part of a whole.
You can compare fractions to see which part is greater.

Step 1 Use a fraction strip to show Gavin's rope. Shade one of the equal parts.	The rope is divided into 4 equal parts. Gavin uses $\frac{1}{4}$.
Step 2 Use a fraction strip to show Marco's rope. Shade one of the equal parts.	The rope is divided into 8 equal parts. Marco uses $\frac{1}{8}$.
Step 3 Compare the fractions. Which fraction strip shows more shading? Circle the fraction. The circled fraction shows the greater part of the whole.	$\frac{1}{4}$ $\frac{1}{8}$ $\frac{1}{4}$ $>$ $\frac{1}{8}$

So, __Gavin__ uses more rope.

REASONING Why is it important that Gavin's rope and Marco's rope are the same size? Explain.

Possible response: if the ropes were different sizes, you
couldn't compare the parts. A smaller fraction of a bigger
whole could be the same size as a bigger fraction of a
smaller whole.

1. Liza and Becca each have equal-sized ribbons. Liza uses $\frac{1}{3}$ of her ribbon to decorate a notebook. Becca uses $\frac{1}{6}$ of her ribbon to decorate a notebook. Who uses more ribbon?

Remember
The fraction strip with more shading shows the greater fraction.

- Shade the first fraction strip to show $\frac{1}{3}$.
- Shade the second fraction strip to show $\frac{1}{6}$. $\frac{1}{3}$
- Which fraction shows more shading, $\frac{1}{3}$ or $\frac{1}{6}$?
- Write > or < to make the sentence true.

$\frac{1}{3}$ $>$ $\frac{1}{6}$

So, __Liza__ uses more ribbon.

Circle the greater fraction.

2. $\frac{1}{10}$ 3. $\frac{1}{2}$

$\frac{1}{8}$ $\frac{1}{6}$

Problem Solving • Show Your Work

Shade the fraction strips to show the fractions.
Circle the greater fraction.

4. $\frac{1}{4}$ 5. $\frac{1}{12}$

$\frac{1}{2}$ $\frac{1}{4}$

6. How does the size of the fraction change as the bottom number changes?

Possible response: as the bottom number gets bigger,
the size of the fraction gets smaller. The more equal
parts of the whole there are, the smaller each part is.

Name _____

Learn the Math

Gavin and Marco each have equal-sized pieces of rope. Gavin uses $\frac{1}{4}$ of his rope for an art project. Marco uses $\frac{1}{8}$ of his rope for an art project. Who uses more rope?

A fraction can name a part of a whole.
You can compare fractions to see which part is greater.

Step 1 Use a fraction strip to show Gavin's rope. Shade one of the equal parts.	The rope is divided into 4 equal parts. Gavin uses $\frac{1}{4}$.
Step 2 Use a fraction strip to show Marco's rope. Shade one of the equal parts.	The rope is divided into 8 equal parts. Marco uses $\frac{1}{8}$.
Step 3 Compare the fractions. Which fraction strip shows more shading? Circle the fraction. The circled fraction shows the greater part of the whole.	$\frac{1}{4}$ $\frac{1}{8}$ $\frac{1}{4} \bigcirc \frac{1}{8}$

So, _____ uses more rope.

REASONING Why is it important that Gavin's rope and Marco's rope are the same size? Explain.

_____

_____

_____

1. Liza and Becca each have equal-sized ribbons. Liza uses $\frac{1}{3}$ of her ribbon to decorate a notebook. Becca uses $\frac{1}{6}$ of her ribbon to decorate a notebook. Who uses more ribbon?

> **Remember**
> The fraction strip with more shading shows the greater fraction.

- Shade the first fraction strip to show $\frac{1}{3}$.

- Shade the second fraction strip to show $\frac{1}{6}$.

- Which fraction shows more shading, $\frac{1}{3}$ or $\frac{1}{6}$? _____

- Write > or < to make the sentence true.

   $\frac{1}{3}$ ◯ $\frac{1}{6}$

So, _____ uses more ribbon.

Circle the greater fraction.

2. $\frac{1}{10}$

   $\frac{1}{8}$

3. $\frac{1}{2}$

   $\frac{1}{6}$

Problem Solving • Show Your Work

Shade the fraction strips to show the fractions.
Circle the greater fraction.

4. $\frac{1}{4}$

   $\frac{1}{2}$

5. $\frac{1}{12}$

   $\frac{1}{4}$

6. How does the size of the fraction change as the bottom number changes?

   _____

   _____

   _____

Objective
To read, write, and model fractional parts of a whole

Vocabulary
fraction A number that names part of a whole or part of a group

numerator The part of a fraction above the line, which tells how many parts are being counted

denominator The part of a fraction below the line, which tells how many equal parts there are in the whole or in the group

Manipulatives
fraction tiles
fraction circles

COMMON ERRORS

- Students may count the equal parts or the shaded parts incorrectly.

- To correct this, have them put a small x on the parts that they have already counted so they know not to count them again.

Learn the Math page IN147 Discuss the question with students.

Guide students through Step 1. Ask: **How many equal parts are there?** 10

For Step 2, ask: **How many shaded parts are there?** 3

For Step 3, discuss what the numerator is and what the denominator is.

REASONING Discuss the question with students. As a class, count all of the parts and then count all of the parts that are not shaded.

Do the Math page IN148 Discuss Exercise 1 with students. Ask: **What are you trying to find out?** what fraction of the parallelogram Linda shaded

Guide students to solve the problem.

Ask: **Does it matter that the shaded parts are not together? Why or why not?** No, it does not matter. Even though they are not together, they are still part of the whole.

Assign Exercises 2–6 and monitor students' work.

Discuss Problem 7 with students. Explain how there can be multiple ways to find a solution to a problem.

Students who make more than 3 errors in Exercises 1–7 may benefit from the **Alternative Teaching Strategy.**

Alternative Teaching Strategy
Call 10 students up to the front of the classroom. Arrange them in a line across the front of the room.

Say: **Think of these ten students as the whole. Each student is one equal part.** Ask: **How many of these 10 students have brown hair?** Answers will vary. Have the students with brown hair step forward. **What fraction of these students have brown hair?** Answers will vary. Have the brown-haired students step back.

Continue asking questions about appropriate characteristics. The answers should always be fractions with the denominator of 10, or tenths.

Learn the Math

The bar is divided into equal parts. What fraction of the bar is shaded?

Step 1	
Count the equal parts.	↑↑↑↑↑↑↑↑↑↑ 1 2 3 4 5 6 7 8 9 10 There are 10 equal parts.
Step 2	
Count the shaded parts.	↑↑↑ 1 2 3 There are 3 shaded parts.
Step 3	
Write the fraction.	shaded parts → $\frac{3}{10}$ ← numerator total parts → ← denominator The fraction is $\frac{3}{10}$, or three tenths.

So, $\frac{3}{10}$, or **three tenths** of the bar is shaded.

REASONING What fraction of the bar is not shaded? Explain your answer.

Possible response: $\frac{7}{10}$ **of the bar is not shaded.**

There are 10 equal parts and 7 are not shaded.

Do the Math

1. Linda shades equal parts of this parallelogram. What fraction of the parallelogram does she shade?

- How many equal parts are in the parallelogram? __10__
- How many parts are shaded? __4__
- What fraction is shaded? $\frac{4}{10}$
- Linda shades $\frac{4}{10}$ of the parallelogram.
- The fraction in words is **four tenths**

Write a fraction for the shaded part.

2. $\frac{1}{10}$

3. $\frac{6}{10}$

4. $\frac{5}{10}$

Problem Solving • Show Your Work

Use the pictures to solve.

5. Ms. Lin's class gets a pizza that is divided into equal slices. They eat several of the slices. What fraction of the pizza do they eat?

$\frac{7}{10}$, or seven tenths

6. Cindy draws a design on the cover of her notebook. She draws a bar with equal pieces and shades some of the pieces. What fraction of the bar does she shade?

$\frac{2}{10}$, or two tenths

7. In Problem 6, describe two ways Cindy can find how many bars are not shaded.

Possible response: Cindy can subtract 2 from 10 to find

that 8 bars are not shaded. She can also count the bars

that are not shaded.

Name _____

Learn the Math

The bar is divided into equal parts. What fraction of the bar is shaded?

Step 1 Count the equal parts.	There are 10 equal parts.
Step 2 Count the shaded parts.	There are 3 shaded parts.
Step 3 Write the fraction.	shaded parts → $\frac{3}{10}$ ← numerator total parts ← denominator The fraction is $\frac{3}{10}$, or three tenths.

So, $\frac{}{}$, or _____ of the bar is shaded.

REASONING What fraction of the bar is not shaded? Explain your answer.

_____

_____

1. Linda shades equal parts of this parallelogram.
What fraction of the parallelogram does she shade?

- How many equal parts are in the parallelogram? _____

- How many parts are shaded? _____

- What fraction is shaded? _____

- Linda shades _____ of the parallelogram.

- The fraction in words is _____.

Write a fraction for the shaded part.

2. **3.** **4.**

Problem Solving • Show Your Work

Use the pictures to solve.

5. Ms. Lin's class gets a pizza that is divided into equal slices. They eat several of the slices. What fraction of the pizza do they eat?

6. Cindy draws a design on the cover of her notebook. She draws a bar with equal pieces and shades some of the pieces. What fraction of the bar does she shade?

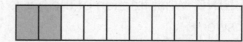

_____   _____

7. In Problem 6, describe two ways Cindy can find how many bars are not shaded.

_____

_____

Read and Write Fractions

Skill 36

Objective
To identify, read, and write fractions

Vocabulary
fraction A number that names part of a whole or part of a group

numerator The part of a fraction above the line, which tells how many parts are being counted

denominator The part of a fraction below the line, which tells how many equal parts there are in the whole or in the group

COMMON ERROR

- Students may incorrectly write the denominator of a fraction.

- To correct this, remind them that the denominator is the total number of equal parts in the whole or in the group.

Learn the Math page IN151 Discuss Example 1 with students. Explain that both fractions have the same denominator. The numerators are different because there are 2 unshaded parts and 1 shaded part. Have students read the fractions as two thirds and one third.

Discuss that the model in Example 2 shows parts of a group and that the model in Example 1 shows parts of a whole. Ask: **What is the denominator in Example 2?** 12 **How many parts are shaded?** 5 **What fraction does this represent?** $\frac{5}{12}$ **How many parts are not shaded?** 7 **What fraction does this represent?** $\frac{7}{12}$

REASONING Elicit that Lucas used the number of unshaded parts as the denominator. He should have used the total number of parts.

Do the Math page IN152 Guide students through Exercise 1. Remind them to count the total number of parts for the denominator.

Assign Exercises 2–7 and monitor students' work.

Discuss Problem 8. Remind students that their pictures of one third can be shown with the shaded or the unshaded part of the model. Encourage them to share their pictures with the class.

Students who make more than 2 errors in Exercises 1–8 may benefit from the **Alternative Teaching Strategy.**

Alternative Teaching Strategy
Manipulatives and Materials: two-color counters, cut-outs of squares and circles

To model fractions of a whole, give each student 3 cut-outs of squares and 3 cut-outs of circles. Have them fold one of the cut-out squares in half, one in thirds, and the other in fourths. Have students shade one or more parts of each square. Ask them to identify the fraction represented by the shaded and the unshaded parts. Repeat with the circle cut-outs.

To model fractions of a group, give each student 12 counters. Ask them to count out 8 counters and then show 3 red counters and 5 yellow counters. Ask: **What fraction is represented by the red counters?** $\frac{3}{8}$ **What fraction is represented by the yellow counters?** $\frac{5}{8}$ Repeat with other fractions.

Learn the Math

Name _____

A **fraction** is a number that names part of a whole or part of a group. The **numerator** tells how many parts are being counted. The **denominator** tells how many equal parts are in the whole or in the group.

Example 1

Write a fraction to name the shaded part.

1 shaded part → $\dfrac{1}{3}$ ← numerator ← denominator

Write a fraction to name the unshaded part.

unshaded parts → $\dfrac{2}{3}$ ← numerator
equal parts in all → ← denominator

Example 2

Write a fraction to name the shaded part.

shaded part → $\dfrac{5}{12}$ ← numerator
equal parts in all → ← denominator

Write a fraction to name the unshaded part.

unshaded parts → $\dfrac{7}{12}$ ← numerator
equal parts in all → ← denominator

REASONING What's the error? Lucas says that $\frac{5}{7}$ names the shaded part in Example 2. Describe his error.

Possible answer: Lucas used the number of unshaded parts as the denominator. He should have used the total number of parts, 12.

Response to Intervention • Tier 2 **IN151**

Do the Math

1. Write a fraction for the shaded part. Write a fraction for the unshaded part.

- How many equal parts are there? __8__
- How many shaded parts are there? __3__
- How many unshaded parts are there? __5__

Shaded parts: $\dfrac{3}{8}$ Unshaded parts: $\dfrac{5}{8}$

Write a fraction for the shaded part. Write a fraction for the unshaded part.

2. shaded parts → $\boxed{1}$
   equal parts in all → $\boxed{4}$
   unshaded parts → $\boxed{3}$
   equal parts in all → $\boxed{4}$

3. shaded parts → $\boxed{2}$
   equal parts in all → $\boxed{5}$
   unshaded parts → $\boxed{3}$
   equal parts in all → $\boxed{5}$

4. shaded: $\dfrac{1}{6}$
   unshaded: $\dfrac{5}{6}$

5. shaded: $\dfrac{4}{5}$
   unshaded: $\dfrac{1}{5}$

6. shaded: $\dfrac{1}{2}$
   unshaded: $\dfrac{1}{2}$

7. shaded: $\dfrac{3}{4}$
   unshaded: $\dfrac{1}{4}$

8. Describe how you can draw a picture to represent the fraction one third. Draw your picture below.

Possible answer: I can draw 3 circles and shade 1 of them. The shaded part of the model would represent one third. Check students' drawings.

IN152 Response to Intervention • Tier 2

Name _____

Learn the Math

A **fraction** is a number that names part of a whole or part of a group. The **numerator** tells how many parts are being counted. The **denominator** tells how many equal parts are in the whole or in the group.

Example 1

Write a fraction to name the shaded part.

1 shaded part   → $\dfrac{1}{3}$ ← numerator

3 equal parts in all →   ← denominator

Write a fraction to name the unshaded part.

unshaded parts   → ☐ ← numerator

equal parts in all → ☐ ← denominator

Example 2

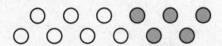

Write a fraction to name the shaded part.

shaded part   → ☐ ← numerator

equal parts in all → ☐ ← denominator

Write a fraction to name the unshaded part.

unshaded parts   → ☐ ← numerator

equal parts in all → ☐ ← denominator

REASONING What's the error? Lucas says that $\dfrac{5}{7}$ names the shaded part in Example 2. Describe his error.

_____

_____

1. Write a fraction for the shaded part. Write a fraction for the unshaded part.

- How many equal parts are there? _____

- How many shaded parts are there? _____

- How many unshaded parts are there? _____

- Shaded parts: _____ Unshaded parts: _____

Write a fraction for the shaded part. Write a fraction for the unshaded part.

2. shaded parts → ☐

   equal parts in all → ☐

   unshaded parts → ☐

   equal parts in all → ☐

3. shaded parts → ☐

   equal parts in all → ☐

   unshaded parts → ☐

   equal parts in all → ☐

4. shaded: _____

   unshaded: _____

5. shaded: _____

   unshaded: _____

6. shaded: _____

   unshaded: _____

7. shaded: _____

   unshaded: _____

8. Describe how you can draw a picture to represent the fraction one third. Draw your picture below.

_____

_____

Parts of a Whole
Skill 37

Objective
To identify and write fractional parts of a whole

Vocabulary

fraction A number that names part of a whole or part of a group

numerator The part of a fraction above the line, which tells how many parts are being counted

denominator The part of a fraction below the line, which tells how many equal parts there are in the whole or in the group

COMMON ERROR

- Students may write the number of parts not shaded as the denominator.

- To correct this, have students first identify how many equal parts are in the whole before counting the number of shaded parts.

Learn the Math page IN155 Read the problem aloud to students. Have students shade the model to show the number of slices of pizza that Brock eats. Ask: **How many parts do you shade?** 3 parts **What fraction of the model is shaded?** $\frac{3}{4}$

Discuss Example 2. Ask: **Which part of the model are you counting for this problem?** the part of the model that is not shaded **How many parts are not shaded?** 1 part **What fraction of the model is not shaded?** $\frac{1}{4}$

REASONING Remind students that the denominator of a fraction is equal to the total number of equal parts in a whole. Encourage students to count the total number of equal parts before counting the number of shaded parts when writing fractions.

Do the Math page IN156 Assist students as they draw a model for Exercise 1. Ask: **Into how many equal parts do you divide the whole?** 8 equal parts **How many parts do you shade?** 1 part **What fraction of the pie does Mrs. Atkin's son eat?** $\frac{1}{8}$ Assign Exercises 2–7 and monitor students' work.

Discuss Problem 8. Ask: **How does the word *not* change this problem from Exercises 2–7?** Possible answer: For Problem 8, I count the number of parts that are not shaded. For Exercises 2–7, I count the number of parts that are shaded.

Students who make more than 2 errors in Exercises 1–8 may benefit from the **Alternative Teaching Strategy.**

Alternative Teaching Strategy
Manipulatives: fraction circles

Give pairs of students one set of fraction circles. Have them model a whole by placing $\frac{1}{4}$ fraction pieces on the whole fraction circle. Ask: **How many equal parts are there?** 4 equal parts Have students take away 1 of the pieces. Ask: **What fraction does the model show now?** $\frac{3}{4}$ Have students model a whole using $\frac{1}{8}$ fraction pieces. Ask: **How many equal parts are there?** 8 equal parts Have students take away 3 of the pieces. Ask: **What fraction does the model show now?** $\frac{5}{8}$ Repeat the activity with other fractions.

© Houghton Mifflin Harcourt Publishing Company

Learn the Math

Brock orders a personal-sized pizza for lunch. He eats 3 out of the 4 equal parts. What fraction of the pizza does he eat?

A **fraction** is a number that names part of a whole or part of a group. The **numerator** tells how many parts are being counted. The **denominator** tells how many equal parts are in the whole or in the group.

Example 1

You can draw a model to show the pizza and divide it into 4 equal parts. Shade 3 out of the 4 equal parts.

3 shaded parts → $\frac{3}{4}$ ← numerator
4 equal parts in all → ← denominator

Read: three fourths   Write: $\frac{3}{4}$

So, Brock eats $\frac{3}{4}$ of the pizza.

Example 2

What fraction of the pizza is left?

Look at the part that is not shaded.

part not shaded → $\boxed{1}$ ← numerator
equal parts in all → $\boxed{4}$ ← denominator

So, $\frac{1}{4}$ of the pizza is left.

REASONING What's the error? Justin says that $\frac{2}{4}$ names the shaded part. Describe his error. Write the correct fraction.

Possible answer: Justin used the number of parts not shaded as the denominator. There are 6 equal parts and 2 are shaded. So, $\frac{2}{6}$ is the correct fraction.

Response to Intervention • Tier 2 **IN155**

Do the Math

1. Mrs. Atkins bakes an apple pie and cuts it into 8 equal slices. Her son eats one slice. What fraction of the pie does he eat?

- How many equal parts are there? ___8___
- How many parts are being counted? ___1___
- Draw a model to show the equal parts and shade the parts being counted.

He eats $\frac{1}{8}$ of the pie.

Write a fraction for each shaded part.

2. shaded part → $\boxed{1}$
equal parts in all → $\boxed{2}$

3. shaded parts → $\boxed{7}$
equal parts in all → $\boxed{8}$

4. $\frac{4}{4}$, or 1

5. $\frac{1}{3}$

6. $\frac{5}{8}$

7. $\frac{2}{4}$, or $\frac{1}{2}$

8. What fraction of the circle is not shaded? $\frac{6}{8}$, or $\frac{3}{4}$

IN156 Response to Intervention • Tier 2

Name _____

Learn the Math

Brock orders a personal-sized pizza for lunch. He eats 3 out of the 4 equal parts. What fraction of the pizza does he eat?

A **fraction** is a number that names part of a whole or part of a group. The **numerator** tells how many parts are being counted. The **denominator** tells how many equal parts are in the whole or in the group.

Vocabulary

fraction
numerator
denominator

Example 1

You can draw a model to show the pizza and divide it into 4 equal parts. Shade 3 out of the 4 equal parts.

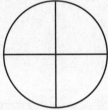

3 shaded parts $\longrightarrow$ $\dfrac{3}{4}$ $\longleftarrow$ numerator

4 equal parts in all $\longrightarrow$ $\longleftarrow$ denominator

Read: three fourths   Write: $\dfrac{3}{4}$

So, Brock eats _____ of the pizza.

Example 2

What fraction of the pizza is left?

Look at the part that is not shaded.

part not shaded $\longrightarrow$ ☐ $\longleftarrow$ numerator

equal parts in all $\longrightarrow$ ☐ $\longleftarrow$ denominator

So, _____ of the pizza is left.

REASONING What's the error? Justin says that $\dfrac{2}{4}$ names the shaded part. Describe his error. Write the correct fraction.

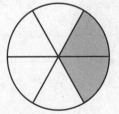

_____

_____

1. Mrs. Atkins bakes an apple pie and cuts it into 8 equal slices. Her son eats one slice. What fraction of the pie does he eat?

- How many equal parts are there? _____

- How many parts are being counted? _____

- Draw a model to show the equal parts and shade the parts being counted.

He eats _____ of the pie.

Write a fraction for each shaded part.

2. 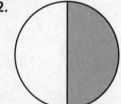   shaded part ⟶ ☐
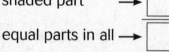   equal parts in all ⟶ ☐

3. 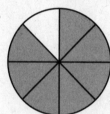   shaded parts ⟶ ☐
equal parts in all ⟶ ☐

4. 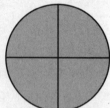   _____

5. 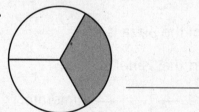   _____

6. 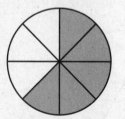   _____

7. 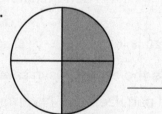   _____

8. What fraction of the circle is not shaded?

_____

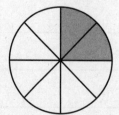

Objective

To identify, read, and write fractions greater than 1 as mixed numbers

Vocabulary

mixed number A number represented by a whole number and a fraction

COMMON ERROR

- Students may have difficulty writing fractions greater than 1 as mixed numbers.

- To correct this, have students first model the fraction greater than 1. Have them count to find the number of parts in each whole. Then have them count the number of shaded wholes and parts and write the mixed number.

Learn the Math page IN159 Read the problem aloud to students. Ask: **How many $\frac{1}{4}$ parts do you need to shade?** 5 Instruct students to shade 5 of the $\frac{1}{4}$ parts. Remind them that a fraction which has the same number in the numerator as in the denominator is equal to 1. Direct students to look at the fraction circle which is completely shaded. Explain that since $\frac{4}{4} = 1$, then $\frac{5}{4}$ is equal to $1 + \frac{1}{4}$, or $1\frac{1}{4}$. Have students read the mixed number as one and one fourth.

REASONING Remind students to first find the number of equal parts into which each shape is divided and to use that number as the denominator. Then they should count the number of parts that are not shaded and write that number as the numerator.

Do the Math page IN160 Guide students through Exercise 1. Ask: **Into how many parts is each whole divided?** 2 Have students count the number of shaded and unshaded parts. Ask: **What fraction greater than 1 represents the number of shaded parts?** $\frac{7}{2}$ **How do you write $\frac{7}{2}$ as a mixed number?** $3\frac{1}{2}$ **What fraction represents the part that is unshaded?** $\frac{1}{2}$

Assign Exercises 2–5 and monitor students' work.

Discuss Problem 6. Ask: **How can you draw a model to show $2\frac{1}{2}$?** Possible answer: I can draw and shade 2 triangles divided into halves, then draw another triangle divided into halves and shade 1 of the 2 parts. **How many of the halves are shaded?** 5 **What fraction greater than 1 does this represent?** $\frac{5}{2}$

Students who make more than 1 error in Exercises 1–6 may benefit from the **Alternative Teaching Strategy**.

Alternative Teaching Strategy

Manipulatives: pattern blocks

Arrange students in groups of 3. Give each student a set of pattern blocks. Direct groups to model $1\frac{4}{6}$ using 2 hexagons and 4 triangles. Have them place the 4 triangles on top of one of the hexagons. Explain that the uncovered hexagon represents the whole number and that the 4 triangles represent the fraction $\frac{4}{6}$. Ask: **How can you use the pattern blocks to model the mixed number as a fraction greater than 1?** Possible answer: Cover the uncovered hexagon with 6 triangles. Ask: **What is $1\frac{4}{6}$ as a fraction greater than 1?** $\frac{10}{6}$ Repeat the activity to make mixed numbers with other pattern blocks.

Learn the Math

Name _____

Mrs. Suarez is baking muffins for the school bake sale. Each batch of muffins uses $\frac{1}{4}$ cup of sugar. How many cups of sugar will she use if she makes 5 batches?

Vocabulary

mixed number

Example 1

You can make a model to find the amount of sugar Mrs. Suarez will use.

Shade $\frac{1}{4}$ for each $\frac{1}{4}$ cup of sugar she will use. Count the number of shaded parts.

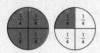

Five parts are shaded.

So, there are $\frac{5}{4}$ in all.

Remember: $\frac{4}{4} = 1$

$\frac{5}{4} = \frac{4}{4} + \frac{1}{4}$

$\frac{5}{4} = 1 + \frac{1}{4} = 1\frac{1}{4}$

So, Mrs. Suarez will use $\frac{5}{4}$, or $1\frac{1}{4}$ cups of sugar.

The number $\frac{5}{4}$ is a fraction greater than 1. A fraction greater than 1 has a numerator that is greater than its denominator.

The number $1\frac{1}{4}$ is a mixed number. A **mixed number** is made up of a whole number and a fraction.

REASONING What fraction is represented by the unshaded part of the model? Explain your answer.

$\frac{3}{4}$; Possible answer: Each whole is divided into 4 equal parts. There are 3 parts that are not shaded.

Response to Intervention • Tier 2 **IN159**

Do the Math

Skill 38

1. Write a mixed number for the shaded part. Write a fraction for the unshaded part.

- Each whole is divided into **halves**.
- How many $\frac{1}{2}$ parts are shaded? **7**
- How many $\frac{1}{2}$ parts are unshaded? **1**

So, $\frac{7}{2}$, or $3\frac{1}{2}$ are shaded, and $\frac{1}{2}$ is unshaded.

Remember
- Count the number of parts in the whole.
- Count the number of shaded or unshaded parts.
- Write a mixed number for a fraction greater than 1.

Write a fraction greater than 1 and a mixed number for the shaded part. Write a fraction for the unshaded part.

2.

shaded: $\frac{12}{5}$, or $2\frac{2}{5}$

unshaded: $\frac{3}{5}$

3.

shaded: $\frac{4}{3}$, or $1\frac{1}{3}$

unshaded: $\frac{2}{3}$

4.

shaded: $\frac{11}{8}$, or $1\frac{3}{8}$

unshaded: $\frac{5}{8}$

5.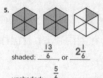

shaded: $\frac{13}{6}$, or $2\frac{1}{6}$

unshaded: $\frac{5}{6}$

6. Write the mixed number $2\frac{1}{2}$ as a fraction greater than 1. Draw a model and shade the parts.

$\frac{5}{2}$; Check students' drawings.

IN160 Response to Intervention • Tier 2

© Houghton Mifflin Harcourt Publishing Company

Name _____

Learn the Math

Mrs. Suarez is baking muffins for the school bake sale. Each batch of muffins uses $\frac{1}{4}$ cup of sugar. How many cups of sugar will she use if she makes 5 batches?

Vocabulary
mixed number

Example 1

You can make a model to find the amount of sugar Mrs. Suarez will use.

Shade $\frac{1}{4}$ for each $\frac{1}{4}$ cup of sugar she will use. Count the number of shaded parts.

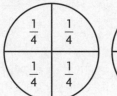

_____ parts are shaded.

So, there are $\frac{5}{4}$ in all.

Remember: $\frac{4}{4} = 1$

$$\frac{5}{4} = \frac{4}{4} + \frac{1}{4}$$

$$\frac{5}{4} = 1 + \frac{1}{4} = 1\frac{1}{4}$$

So, Mrs. Suarez will use _____, or _____ cups of sugar.

The number $\frac{5}{4}$ is a fraction greater than 1. A fraction greater than 1 has a numerator that is greater than its denominator.

The number $1\frac{1}{4}$ is a mixed number. A **mixed number** is made up of a whole number and a fraction.

REASONING What fraction is represented by the unshaded part of the model? Explain your answer.

_____

_____

1. Write a mixed number for the shaded part.
   Write a fraction for the unshaded part.

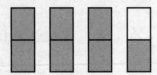

- Each whole is divided into _____.

- How many $\frac{1}{2}$ parts are shaded? _____

- How many $\frac{1}{2}$ parts are unshaded? _____

So, $\dfrac{\boxed{}}{2}$, or _____ are shaded, and $\dfrac{\boxed{}}{2}$
is unshaded.

Remember

- Count the number of parts in the whole.
- Count the number of shaded or unshaded parts.
- Write a mixed number for a fraction greater than 1.

**Write a fraction greater than 1 and a mixed number
for the shaded part. Write a fraction for the unshaded part.**

2.

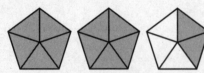

shaded: $\dfrac{\boxed{}}{5}$, or _____

unshaded: $\dfrac{\boxed{}}{5}$

3.

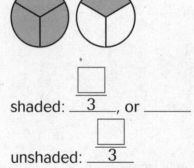

shaded: $\dfrac{\boxed{}}{3}$, or _____

unshaded: $\dfrac{\boxed{}}{3}$

4.

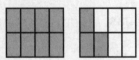

shaded: _____, or _____

unshaded: _____

5.

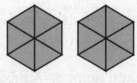

shaded: _____, or _____

unshaded: _____

6. Write the mixed number $2\frac{1}{2}$ as a fraction greater than 1.
   Draw a model and shade the parts.

_____

Objective
To identify the number of sides in two-dimensional shapes

Vocabulary
side A straight line segment in a polygon

COMMON ERROR

- Students may have difficulty keeping track of where they began when counting sides.

- To correct this, have students mark each side as they count. This way, they will know which sides they have already counted.

Learn the Math page IN163 Read and discuss the problem with students. Guide them through Step 1. Count the number of sides in each shape with students. To keep track of the sides, have students mark each side as they count.

For Step 2, ask: **Which shapes have 4 sides?** the trapezoid, the square, and the rectangle **Which are the shapes that Carly will not collect?** the triangles

REASONING Discuss the problem with students. Ask them to explain how a rectangle and a trapezoid are alike and how they are different.

Do the Math page IN164 Discuss Exercise 1 with students. Ask: **Which shapes have exactly 4 sides?** the square,

the trapezoid **Is there a shape with more than 4 sides?** yes Point out that Simon only wants to use shapes with less than 4 sides. Guide students to count the sides of each shape and cross out the shapes that have 4 or more sides. Students should determine that Simon will only use the triangles.

Assign Exercises 2–9 and monitor students' work.

Discuss Problem 10 with students. Ask: **How many sides does one triangle have?** 3 **How many triangles does Belinda draw?** 4 triangles **How many sides do Belinda's triangles have in all?** 12 sides Guide students to explain how they counted the 12 sides. If needed, guide students to use repeated addition or skip counting to find the number of sides in all.

Students who make more than 2 errors in Exercises 1–10 may benefit from the **Alternative Teaching Strategy**.

Alternative Teaching Strategy
Materials: toothpicks

Give each student some toothpicks. Tell them that they are going to use the toothpicks to model two-dimensional shapes. Draw a picture of a shape on the board and have students model the shape using their toothpicks. For shapes with different side lengths, encourage students to use more than one toothpick for longer sides. Ask: **How many sides does this shape have?** When a variety of shapes have been modeled, have students work in pairs to create and draw shapes with 5, 6, 7, and 8 straight sides.

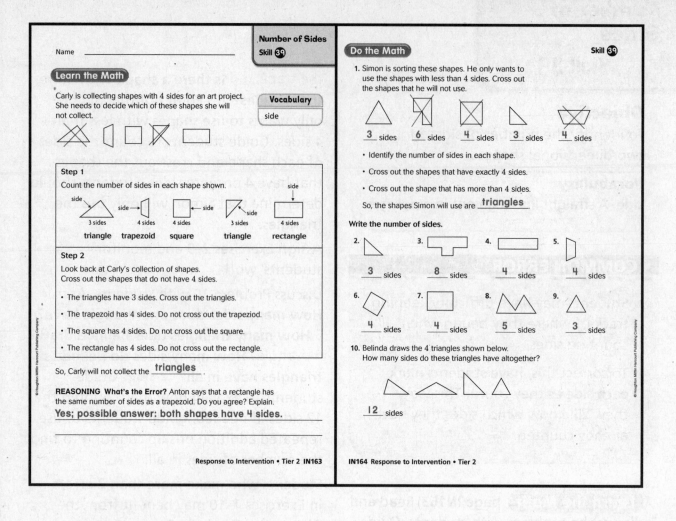

Name _____

Learn the Math

Carly is collecting shapes with 4 sides for an art project. She needs to decide which of these shapes she will not collect.

Vocabulary

side

Step 1

Count the number of sides in each shape shown.

| triangle | trapezoid | square | triangle | rectangle |
| 3 sides | 4 sides | 4 sides | 3 sides | 4 sides |

Step 2

Look back at Carly's collection of shapes.
Cross out the shapes that do not have 4 sides.

• The triangles have 3 sides. Cross out the triangles.

• The trapezoid has 4 sides. Do not cross out the trapeziod.

• The square has 4 sides. Do not cross out the square.

• The rectangle has 4 sides. Do not cross out the rectangle.

So, Carly will not collect the _triangles_ .

REASONING What's the Error? Anton says that a rectangle has the same number of sides as a trapezoid. Do you agree? Explain.
Yes; possible answer: both shapes have 4 sides.

Response to Intervention • Tier 2 **IN163**

Do the Math

Skill 39

1. Simon is sorting these shapes. He only wants to use the shapes with less than 4 sides. Cross out the shapes that he will not use.

  _3_ sides   _6_ sides   _4_ sides   _3_ sides   _4_ sides

• Identify the number of sides in each shape.

• Cross out the shapes that have exactly 4 sides.

• Cross out the shape that has more than 4 sides.

So, the shapes Simon will use are _triangles_

Write the number of sides.

2. _3_ sides
3. _8_ sides
4. _4_ sides
5. _4_ sides

6. _4_ sides
7. _4_ sides
8. _5_ sides
9. _3_ sides

10. Belinda draws the 4 triangles shown below. How many sides do these triangles have altogether?

  _12_ sides

IN164 Response to Intervention • Tier 2

Name _____

Learn the Math

Carly is collecting shapes with 4 sides for an art project.
She needs to decide which of these shapes she will
not collect.

Vocabulary

side

Step 1

Count the number of sides in each shape shown.

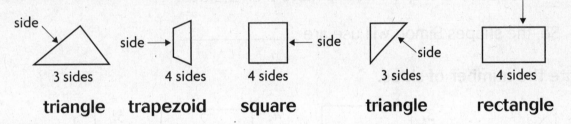

triangle   trapezoid   square   triangle   rectangle

Step 2

Look back at Carly's collection of shapes.
Cross out the shapes that do not have 4 sides.

• The triangles have 3 sides. Cross out the triangles.

• The trapezoid has 4 sides. Do not cross out the trapeziod.

• The square has 4 sides. Do not cross out the square.

• The rectangle has 4 sides. Do not cross out the rectangle.

So, Carly will not collect the _____ .

REASONING What's the Error? Anton says that a rectangle has
the same number of sides as a trapezoid. Do you agree? Explain.

_____

_____

1. Simon is sorting these shapes. He only wants to use the shapes with less than 4 sides. Cross out the shapes that he will not use.

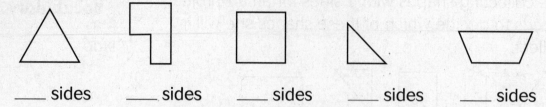

___ sides   ___ sides   ___ sides   ___ sides   ___ sides

- Identify the number of sides in each shape.

- Cross out the shapes that have exactly 4 sides.

- Cross out the shape that has more than 4 sides.

So, the shapes Simon will use are _____.

Write the number of sides.

2.

_____ sides

3.

_____ sides

4.

_____ sides

5.

_____ sides

6.

_____ sides

7.

_____ sides

8.

_____ sides

9.

_____ sides

10. Belinda draws the 4 triangles shown below. How many sides do these triangles have altogether?

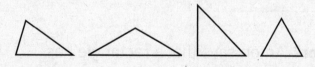

_____ sides

Geometric Patterns
Skill 40

Objective
To identify and predict the next two shapes in repeating patterns

Vocabulary
pattern unit The part of a pattern that repeats

Manipulatives
color tiles, pattern blocks

COMMON ERROR

- Students may have difficulty identifying the pattern unit.

- To correct this, have students say the names of the shapes aloud. The rhythm of the words can help them identify the pattern unit.

Learn the Math page IN167 Guide students through the first example. Help them identify the pattern unit. Then have students say the names of the shapes aloud. Ask: **What is the pattern unit?** triangle, square **How can you decide what comes next?** Possible answer: I can look at the last given shape and the pattern unit to predict the next two shapes, triangle, square.

In the second example, point out that this pattern unit involves three different shapes: square, circle, rectangle. Have students circle the pattern unit and draw the next two shapes in the pattern.

Repeat the process for the third example. Point out that this pattern unit involves three shapes, but one of the shapes is repeated.

REASONING Some students may not recognize the pattern unit. To help with

this, have them build the pattern out of color tiles, using red for tuba and blue for drum.

Do the Math page IN168 Guide the students through Exercise 1. Ask: **How many shapes are in the pattern unit?** 3 **What is the pattern unit?** circle, rectangle, square **Which shape do you need to look at to predict what comes next?** I need to look at the last shape in the pattern, the square.

Assign Exercises 2–6 and monitor students' work.

Read and discuss Problem 7 with students. Have them examine both patterns shown. Ask: **What is the pattern unit for *a*?** square, circle **What is the pattern unit for *b*?** square, square, circle Ask students to predict the next two shapes for each pattern and compare their predictions to Jimmy's prediction. Ask: **At which pattern could Jimmy have been looking?** pattern *a*

Students who make more than 1 error in Exercises 1–7 may benefit from the **Alternative Teaching Strategy**.

Alternative Teaching Strategy
Manipulatives: pattern blocks

Provide each student with a set of pattern blocks. Have them choose two different shapes from the set to use as the pattern unit. Instruct them to place the shapes in a row on their desk. Tell them to use the remaining pattern blocks to repeat the pattern unit three times. Have students switch desks with their neighbor. Their task is to predict the next two shapes in the pattern. Repeat this activity, encouraging students to make pattern units that have three shapes.

Learn the Math

A **pattern unit** helps you predict what comes next in a pattern. It is the part that repeats.

Vocabulary

pattern unit

Circle the pattern unit. Then draw the next two shapes.

The pattern unit is triangle, square.

The next two shapes in the pattern are

triangle , square

The next two shapes in the pattern are

square , circle

The next two shapes in the pattern are

small triangle , large triangle

REASONING In music class, Mr. Thomas lines up students by the instruments they play: tuba, drum, tuba, drum, tuba, drum. What is the pattern unit? Will tuba or drum come next? How do you know?

The pattern unit is tuba, drum. Tuba will come next.

Possible answer: since drum was the last instrument in the pattern, tuba will come next.

Do the Math

Skill 40

1. Kim is making a bracelet with beads using a pattern. Circle the pattern unit. Draw the next two beads Kim will use.

Remember
The pattern unit helps you predict what comes next.

• Identify the pattern unit and circle it.

• Name the next two beads Kim will use.

circle , rectangle

• Draw the next two beads Kim will use:

Circle the pattern unit. Then draw the next two shapes.

2.

3.

4.

5.

6.

7. Jimmy predicted that the next two shapes in a pattern would be square, circle. Identify the pattern below that Jimmy could have been looking at.

a. □○○○□○○○ b. □□○□□○□○○

Jimmy could have been looking at pattern ___a___

Name _____

Learn the Math

A **pattern unit** helps you predict what comes next
in a pattern. It is the part that repeats.

Vocabulary

pattern unit

Circle the pattern unit. Then draw the next two shapes.

The pattern unit is triangle, square.

The next two shapes in the pattern are

       triangle   , _____.

The next two shapes in the pattern are

_____ , _____.

The next two shapes in the pattern are

_____ , _____.

REASONING In music class, Mr. Thomas lines up students by the
instruments they play: tuba, drum, tuba, drum, tuba, drum. What is the
pattern unit? Will tuba or drum come next? How do you know?

_____

_____

_____

1. Kim is making a bracelet with beads using a pattern. Circle the pattern unit. Draw the next two beads Kim will use.

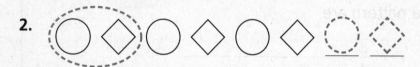

- Identify the pattern unit and circle it.

- Name the next two beads Kim will use.

_____, _____

- Draw the next two beads Kim will use: _____ _____

Circle the pattern unit. Then draw the next two shapes.

2. ◯ ◇ ◯ ◇ ◯ ◇ ◯ ◇

3. ▽ △ ▽ △ ▽ △ ___ ___

4. △◯△ △◯△ △◯△ ___ ___

5. ◇ ◇ ◇ ◇ ◇ ◇ ◇ ◇ ◇ ___ ___

6. ● ◯ ◯ ● ◯ ◯ ● ◯ ◯ ___ ___

7. Jimmy predicted that the next two shapes in a pattern would be square, circle. Identify the pattern below that Jimmy could have been looking at.

   a. ▢◯▢◯▢◯▢◯   b. ▢▢◯▢▢◯▢▢

   Jimmy could have been looking at pattern _____.

Classify Angles
Skill 41

Objective

To classify angles as right angles, acute angles, or obtuse angles

Vocabulary

angle A shape formed by two line segments or rays that share the same endpoint

vertex The point at which two rays of an angle or two (or more) line segments meet in a two dimensional shape

right angle An angle that forms a square corner and has a measure of 90°

acute angle An angle that has a measure greater than 0° and less than 90°

obtuse angle An angle that has a measure greater than 90° and less than 180°

COMMON ERROR

- Students may have difficulties measuring angles that do not have one ray that is horizontal.

- To correct this, encourage students to turn their paper so that one ray of the angle is horizontal.

© Houghton Mifflin Harcourt Publishing Company

Learn the Math page IN171 Begin by having students review the vocabulary terms. Ask: **What is an angle?** a shape formed by two line segments or rays that share a common endpoint Ask: **What are three types of angles?** right angles, acute angles, and obtuse angles

Explain to students how to use a square corner to measure angles. Point out that using a square corner as a guide helps determine whether a specific angle is greater than, less than, or equal to a right angle. Then have students classify the angles on the page.

REASONING Before students answer the question, have them practice classifying angles. Have students identify objects around the classroom that form right angles, acute angles, and obtuse angles. Have students use a sheet of paper to check the angles they find. Then, have students sketch the angles on index cards and label each index card as a reference.

Do the Math page IN172 Read and discuss Exercise 1 with students. Help students see that they should be looking at the angles in the triangles, as well as the angle formed where the two shapes meet.

Assign Exercises 2–9 and monitor students' work.

Discuss Problem 10 with the students. Invite volunteers to answer questions. Ask: **What shape do the hands of a clock form?** They form angles. **What are some times where right angles are formed with the hands of a clock?** Possible answers: 3:00 or 9:00

Students who make more than 2 errors in Exercises 1–10 may benefit from the **Alternative Teaching Strategy**.

Alternative Teaching Strategy

Materials: dot paper

Give students dot paper and have them draw a square. Ask: **How many angles does this figure have?** 4 **How many angles are right angles?** 4 Have students draw a right triangle. **How many angles does this figure have?** 3 **How many angles are right angles?** 1 **How many angles are acute angles?** 2 Have students draw a parallelogram and ask the same questions about its angles. 4 angles; 2 acute; 2 obtuse Repeat with similar problems.

Name _____

Learn the Math

An **angle** is a shape formed by two line segments or rays that share the same endpoint. The shared endpoint is called a **vertex**. There are different types of angles.

right angle	angle marker	angle marker
A **right angle** forms a square corner and measures 90°.	An **acute angle** is less than a right angle. It has a measure greater than 0° and less than 90°.	An **obtuse angle** is greater than a right angle. It has a measure greater than 90° and less than 180°.

Vocabulary

angle
vertex
right angle
acute angle
obtuse angle

Maya looks for examples of angles in her classroom. She draws the three angles below. Which types of angles does Maya draw?

angle 1   angle 2   angle 3

Use the corner of a sheet of paper to tell whether each angle is an *acute angle*, a *right angle*, or an *obtuse angle*.

angle 1 — Angle 1 is   a right angle

angle 2 — Angle 2 is   an acute angle

angle 3 — Angle 3 is   an obtuse angle

REASONING How do you use the corner of a sheet of paper to help you classify an angle?

Possible answer: Line up the vertex of the angle with the corner of the paper, so one ray lines up with the edge. Then see where the other ray lies.

---

1. Marco drew the following picture. How many of each type of angle are shown in Marco's picture?

• What tool can you use to help you classify the angles?
the corner of a piece of paper

• How many of the angles are right angles? __2__

• How many of the angles are acute angles? __4__

• How many of the angles are obtuse angles? __1__

So, in Marco's picture, there are __2__ right angles, __4__ acute angles, and __1__ obtuse angle.

Remember

• Right angles form square corners.
• Acute angles have a measure greater than 0° and less than 90°.
• Obtuse angles have a measure greater than 90° and less than 180°.

Classify each angle. Write *acute*, *right* or *obtuse*.

2.
obtuse angle

3.
right angle

4.
obtuse angle

5.
acute angle

6.
acute angle

7.
right angle

8.
obtuse angle

9.
right angle

10. Give a time when the hands on a clock represent a right angle.
Possible answer: 3:00

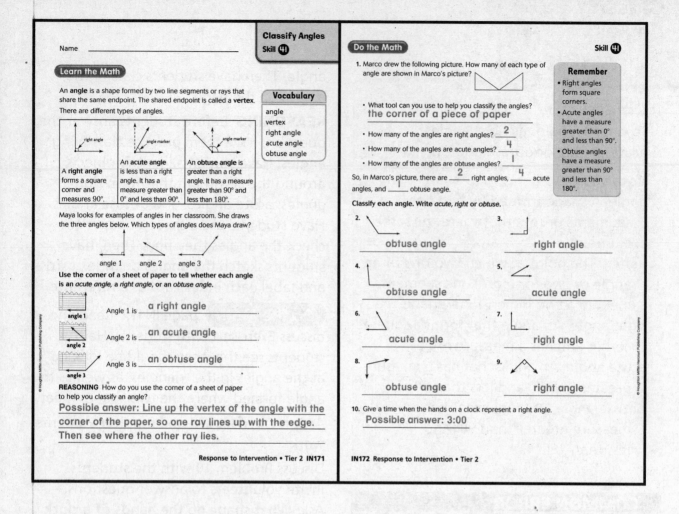

Name _____

Learn the Math

An **angle** is a shape formed by two line segments or rays that share the same endpoint. The shared endpoint is called a **vertex**. There are different types of angles.

Vocabulary

angle
vertex
right angle
acute angle
obtuse angle

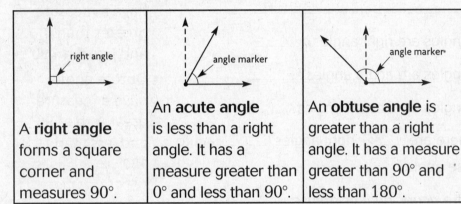

A **right angle** forms a square corner and measures 90°.	An **acute angle** is less than a right angle. It has a measure greater than 0° and less than 90°.	An **obtuse angle** is greater than a right angle. It has a measure greater than 90° and less than 180°.

Maya looks for examples of angles in her classroom. She draws the three angles below. Which types of angles does Maya draw?

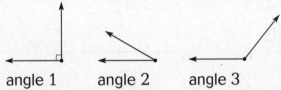

angle 1   angle 2   angle 3

Use the corner of a sheet of paper to tell whether each angle is an *acute angle*, a *right angle*, or an *obtuse angle*.

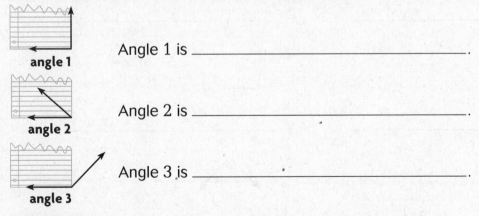

Angle 1 is _____.

Angle 2 is _____.

Angle 3 is _____.

REASONING How do you use the corner of a sheet of paper to help you classify an angle?

_____

_____

_____

1. Marco drew the following picture. How many of each type of angle are shown in Marco's picture?

   • What tool can you use to help you classify the angles?

   _____

   • How many of the angles are right angles? _____

   • How many of the angles are acute angles? _____

   • How many of the angles are obtuse angles? _____

So, in Marco's picture, there are _____ right angles, _____ acute angles, and _____ obtuse angle.

Classify each angle. Write *acute, right* **or** *obtuse.*

2.

_____

3.

_____

4.

_____

5.

_____

6.

_____

7.

_____

8.

_____

9.

_____

10. Give a time when the hands on a clock represent a right angle.

   _____